You're Not the Only One

You're Not the Only One

*Reflections on Faith, Doubt, Growing Up,
and the College Experience*

Megan LeCluyse

WIPF & STOCK · Eugene, Oregon

YOU'RE NOT THE ONLY ONE
Reflections on Faith, Doubt, Growing Up, and the College Experience

Copyright © 2025 Megan LeCluyse. All rights reserved. Except for brief quotations in critical publications or reviews, no part of this book may be reproduced in any manner without prior written permission from the publisher. Write: Permissions, Wipf and Stock Publishers, 199 W. 8th Ave., Suite 3, Eugene, OR 97401.

Wipf & Stock
An Imprint of Wipf and Stock Publishers
199 W. 8th Ave., Suite 3
Eugene, OR 97401

www.wipfandstock.com

PAPERBACK ISBN: 979–8-3852–3762–3
HARDCOVER ISBN: 979–8-3852–3763–0
EBOOK ISBN: 979–8-3852–3764–7

VERSION NUMBER 07/28/25

All Scripture quotations, unless otherwise indicated, are from New Revised Standard Version Bible, copyright © 1989 National Council of Churches of Christ in the United States of America. Used by permission. All rights reserved. friendshippress.org.

Scripture taken from THE MESSAGE. Copyright © 1993, 1994, 1995, 1996, 2000, 2001, 2002. Used by permission of NavPress Publishing Group.

Scripture quotations taken from the (NASB®) New American Standard Bible®, Copyright © 1960, 1971, 1977, 1995, 2020 by The Lockman Foundation. Used by permission. All rights reserved. lockman.org.

Rumi, Quatrains from Open Secret: Versions of Rumi by John Moyne and Coleman Barks. Copyright © 1984 by John Moyne and Coleman Barks. Reprinted by arrangement with The Permissions Company, LLC, on behalf of Shambhala Publications Inc., Boulder, Colorado, shambhala.com.

"Home" from BEAUTY AND THE BEAST: THE BROADWAY MUSICAL
Music by Alan MenkenLyrics by Tim Rice© 1994 Wonderland Music Company, Inc., Menken Music, Trunksong Music Ltd. and Walt Disney Music CompanyAll Rights Reserved. Used by Permission. *Reprinted by Permission of Hal Leonard LLC*

"I Am Moana" (Song of the Ancestors) from MOANA, music by Lin-Manuel Miranda, Opetaia Foa'i and Mark MancinaLyrics by Lin-Manuel Miranda and Opetaia Foa'i© 2016 Walt Disney Music Company and Wonderland Music Company, Inc.All Rights Reserved. Used by Permission.*Reprinted by Permission of Hal Leonard LLC*

For all the students I have and will work with,
and those who go through college wondering
if they are the only person who feels the way they do.

My story is important not because it is mine, God knows, but because if I tell it anything like right, the chances are you will recognize that in many ways it is also yours. . . . It is precisely through these stories in all their particularity, as I have long believed and often said, that God makes himself known to each of us more powerfully and personally. If this is true, it means that to lose track of our stories is to be profoundly impoverished not only humanly but also spiritually.

—Frederick Buechner

Contents

Acknowledgments | *ix*

Introduction | *xi*

1. The Best Four Years of Your Life? | 1
2. Finding a Space to Be Your True Self and Embrace All That You Are | 10
3. Learning to Be True to Yourself, and That It's Okay to Have Water in Your Red Solo Cup | 18
4. There's No Place Like Home | 27
5. When What You Believe Changes | 34
6. Do I Really Want to Call Myself "Christian"? | 42
7. Finding a Faith Community: No Church Is Going to Be Exactly Like Your Home Church | 50
8. Finding Your "Family" | 58
9. Will You Be My Mentor? | 66
10. Loving Yourself | 75
11. Loving Others | 83
12. What Should I Do with My Life? | 90
13. When God Calls You to Go to Unexpected Places or Do Unexpected Things | 98

14 How Am I Going to Get It All Done? (Insert Panic Here) | 105

15 Perfectionism, Self-Expectations, and Being a Workaholic: How to Balance Work, Life, and Play | 113

16 Mind, Body, Soul: Tending to Your Well-Being | 120

17 Owning Your Own Paradox | 128

18 Studying Abroad: When I Was the One with the Accent | 136

19 Engaging with People Who Are Different Than You | 143

20 Why Do Bad Things Happen to Good People? | 151

21 Coming Face-to-Face with Mortality | 158

22 Connecting Across Space and Time: We Are a Part of a Bigger Story | 165

Conclusion | 172

Bibliography | 175

Acknowledgments

THIS BOOK HAS BEEN almost exactly a decade in the making. There have been many people along the way for whom I am grateful.

First, to all the students I have worked with over the years—thank you for sharing your lives and stories with me and letting me be a part of your journey. I am especially grateful for those who let me tell their stories in these pages. Except for those whose writings I have quoted and attributed to them, students' names have been changed, but the stories are real.

This journey began because of two students who told me they wanted to read my book. Thank you, Kathryn and Mary Kate, for helping me to hear God calling me to this project.

In 2020, as our fall semester went virtual, the grad student book group at the Christian Association at the University of Pennsylvania (CA) offered to read my manuscript, which was both immensely helpful and fun. Thank you to Anthony, Ariel, Karen, and Lukas for being a part of this—for some that included reading it again—and an extra thank you to Becca, Gui, and Mauricio for being my accountability buddies over many cups of coffee as I worked to find a publisher and get this out into the world. What you all gave me over Zoom and beyond was a gift and made me a little less nervous to share my work with others.

I also could not tell my story were it not for my own college friends, family, and mentors. Two decades later, I remain so grateful that we met and that our relationships continue. Thank you for seeing me and loving me as I was and am. If I had to relive a year of my life, senior year of college would be pretty high on the list.

Thank you to those at Wipf and Stock for allowing me to share this work with college students who need to know that they aren't the only one

Acknowledgments

feeling whatever it is they are feeling. I am grateful for your patience with me as this first-time author figures this whole thing out!

Finally, thank you Mom, Dad, and Annie for supporting me on this journey. You are the ones who have been in this with me for the whole decade and kept encouraging me to continue. I am especially grateful to my mom, who spent a week on very short notice reading through the manuscript to give me edits as I was finishing it all up and dealing with her daughter who has never mastered the art of not procrastinating. I love you all and am grateful for the ways you have helped shape me into the person I am today.

Introduction

How do I begin to tell you about my college experience? Do I start with my freshman year of college—is that really the place to begin this book? Do I start by mentioning how, after having numerous, well-meaning people tell me I was headed for "the best four years of my life," freshman year was by far the hardest year of my life? I was so anxious I barely ate for the first few weeks. Do I tell you about how classes were fine first semester, but they wouldn't let me, as an English major, sign up for English classes my second semester, so I signed myself up for higher level religious studies courses instead? I wasn't interested in going to big parties and struggled to make friends my freshman year. I often felt lonely. After everything people had told me about how fun college would be, I thought I must be doing something wrong. Is this really where I start?

Or do I begin by telling you about how by senior year I was having a fantastic time at college? I had a wonderful group of friends, three of whom I shared a house with. Do I tell you about how, as I grew in maturity and experience, I got to be in leadership roles and felt a great deal more self-confidence? Do I share how I was taking upper-level courses in subjects I found really interesting and had some fantastic professors? I still wasn't a partyer but would occasionally go out with friends. I was looking ahead towards going to seminary, yet while this was all great, senior year also brought of lot of emotions and ups and downs along with it, too.

Both of these are part of how I begin because I hope this book will meet you wherever you are in your own college journey and provide points of connection. In the following pages, you'll find pieces of my story. You'll also find pieces of other's stories, those I have shared my life with as a daughter, sister, friend, and pastor. They are stories from when I was in

Introduction

college and stories from the years since then. I share them not because you need to know the details of my life, but because I hope in them you find things that resonate with you, that connect with your story. I share them because too often in college we feel like we are alone when we truly are not. I share them because through them I have learned a great deal, and because if I could have read this book while in college, it would have given me hope and assured me I was not the only one who felt this way.

I also hope to connect with your story if you have a wonderful freshman year through some of the many other experiences that college can bring. My freshman year was not my entire college experience, but it was part of the experience. So was meeting people who would become incredibly close friends—family even—during my sophomore and junior years. I studied abroad, took classes that I loved, and developed some fabulous mentorships. I struggled with a desire for my work to be perfect and tried to find balance in my life. I learned how to be more of an adult. In all of this, my faith played a central role, guiding me while also growing and changing with me.

If we're going to be sharing these pages, let me share a little about myself. I began my freshman year at the University of Arizona (U of A) in 2004, a two-hour drive from my family's home in Phoenix, Arizona. I began college with one of the most intense weeks of my life—better known as the Pride of Arizona Marching Band's band camp—baking under the Arizona sun and drinking around six liters of water a day. I was an English major, with minors in history and religious studies. I worked as an usher at the on-campus theatre beginning my sophomore year, and you'll experience my love for musicals tucked into this book. I got involved with the Presbyterian Campus Ministry (PCM) my first week of school, even though I was one of two freshman who attended that year. College was a time of immense growth for me, and growth often means both pain, even tears, as well as a sense of accomplishment, of hindsight allowing you to see where you've come.

I knew when I started college that I would be going to seminary once I graduated, though I did have a season of wrestling with my call as I applied to seminary my senior year. I went to college as someone who already asked a lot of questions about faith and God, and college probably only made me ask more. That's who I am, and, I imagine, who I will always be. Anne Lamott wrote that "the opposite of faith is not doubt, but certainty. Certainty

Introduction

is missing the point entirely. Faith includes noticing the mess".[1] College can be the time when we realize that there is a lot of mess around and have to make sense of what that means. Of course, some days the mess causes me to have major doubts, and others I see God at work in the mess in ways that stop me in my tracks. This book is for those of us who are Christians who are willing to live in the mess and in the grey, to not have the certainty of exact answers or explanations, who want to experience the mystery that is God. I share my story as an invitation to share the journey.

After I finished college, I moved across the country to go to Princeton Theological Seminary, leaving the sunny desert of Arizona for the clouds and snow, along with the legit fall and spring, of New Jersey. Unlike my transition to college, this one went much better, and I immediately felt I was where I was supposed to be. I spent the next four years there, and this was again a season of tremendous personal growth. The growth included a change in what type of ministry I felt called to, one that made me decide to become a campus minister. I have now been serving at the Christian Association at the University of Pennsylvania (Penn) since 2012, and truly believe that this is where God has called me to be for this season of my life. As I was wrestling with my call during my senior year of college, a wise mentor told me that she believed I was indeed called to ministry, to be a minister for those who had lots of questions like me. That is part of what I get to do in my role as a campus minister. I share the college journey with students. Some I get to see from early in their freshman year through graduation, others I meet later on in the journey, still others are grad students, and it is a joy and privilege to be a part of each one of their college experiences.

In the pages that follow, you'll find an exploration of some of the questions and themes that often play a major role while you're in college, along with an invitation to continually make your faith an integrated part of your life and not something you pick up every now and then. The chapters are somewhat arranged in order of transition to college, life at college, and transition out of college. It looks at topics like defining yourself, how to survive at college and beyond, aspirations, and contributions you might make to both your relationships and the wider world. It explores God's sense of call in our lives, and how we live out our own values. Each of our college journeys, while sharing some similar milestones and features, is unique, and so things may not happen for you in the same order I have experienced

---

1. Lamott, *Plan B*, 256–57.

Introduction

them. This book doesn't have to be read from cover to cover, and though you can, it's designed for you to read what you need when you need it. Maybe you read it on your own, maybe you read it with a small group from your campus ministry, or with some friends. In each chapter, you'll find, in addition to my own reflections, a Scripture passage or two, quotes that resonated with me, a prayer, and questions for you to ponder and maybe write responses to or discuss with others.

I hope that this book helps you on your journey of faith while at college, provokes some new thoughts, and allows you to feel a little surer of the child of God you were created to be. I hope as you read that you will know that you are not the only one to have been on this journey; it is a road we travel together.

1

The Best Four Years of Your Life?

THINGS PEOPLE WISHED THEY KNEW IN COLLEGE

I wish I had known that caring for your mental health is as important as your other physical health. I wish I would have known that asking for help is a sign of strength not weakness. And I wish I would have known that there are people who want *real* relationships (both romantic and non-romantic). Search those people out and be ok with letting the others go. —Shavon

In college, I wish I had known that the battles of faith I was fighting (doubting God's call upon my life, feeling like I could not do enough, etc.) would be the foundation for other growth in faith along the next years. That is to say that instead of ignoring my doubts, my fears, or trying to man up and brush them away, I wish I would have engaged with them more deeply to learn something new about grace that God was trying to teach me, but stubborn as I am, it took me years to listen. —Lisa

In college, I wish I knew to get connected to at least one group of people who get me, and who I get. As a shy introvert, I spent much of my first semester in my room. It was miserable. A connection with just one group that met regularly and that would hang together would have made a huge difference in my college experience. —Anna

You're Not the Only One

I wish I would have ignored the constant pressure to have a plan going forward in life. I probably had the clearest five-year plan of anyone in college, but it meant nothing because I wasn't convinced of the plan itself. It just gave my life some structure and I appreciated that. Life doesn't have to be planned or structured in college; just live it, do your best, and find stuff to work hard at. God will make sense of what you learn and what you come to desire. —T. J.

Scripture

Incline your ear, O Lord, and answer me,
for I am poor and needy.
Preserve my life, for I am devoted to you;
save your servant who trusts in you.
You are my God;
be gracious to me, O Lord,
for to you do I cry all day long.
Gladden the soul of your servant,
for to you, O Lord, I lift up my soul.
For you, O Lord, are good and forgiving,
abounding in steadfast love to all who call on you.
Give ear, O Lord, to my prayer;
 listen to my cry of supplication.
In the day of my trouble I call on you,
for you will answer me.
There is none like you among the gods, O Lord,
nor are there any works like yours.
All the nations you have made shall come
and bow down before you, O Lord,
and shall glorify your name.
For you are great and do wondrous things;
you alone are God.
Teach me your way, O Lord,
that I may walk in your truth;
give me an undivided heart to revere your name.
I give thanks to you, O Lord my God, with my whole heart,
and I will glorify your name forever.
For great is your steadfast love toward me;
you have delivered my soul from the depths of Sheol.
(Ps 86:1–13)

The Best Four Years of Your Life?

Part 1: Freshman Year—Ya, That Was Rough

You've probably heard of the "Freshman fifteen."[1] Well let's just say, for me it took on a slightly different meaning than the phrase normally implies. In many ways, freshman year was really hard for me. Sometimes I think it was harder for me than it appears to be for most students. I'm not sure about that though, because while some of you will go to college and begin to feel at home and happy almost immediately, many will not. Others will use various means to numb the pain, namely, alcohol, and that wasn't my scene. When I say that my freshman year was rough, I mean that at one point that spring, following a bout of food poisoning that had taken off a few more pounds, I weighed fifteen pounds *less* than I had when I had left for college.

Let me back up a bit first, back to the months before I left for college. I was lucky to have a lot of adults who cared about me in my life. They were excited to ask about where I was going to college, what my plans were, etc., and many of them would include in the conversation something along the lines of how much I was going to love it and how fun it would be. Some said that college would be the best four years of my life. When people go off to college in the movies, it often seems like it's all happiness and freedom and new school traditions. So, I developed these ideas that what was expected of me was to go to college and love it, while internally feeling a mix of both excitement and a lot of anxiety about the transition that lay ahead. Thankfully, my mom (who was our youth leader at church) gathered those of us headed to college to talk about some of the challenges we would likely experience, the loneliness we would feel, the realities of the transition. Even that conversation couldn't quite prepare me for what was to come.

Something you need to know about me is that when I am really anxious, I can't eat. Sometimes just the anxiety itself can make me throw up, but often, it is triggered when I chew. The first time I remember this manifesting itself was in first grade, when the magician was coming to do a magic show at our school. Magic makes me nervous. I don't like things that I can't understand or explain, or that make me realize I'm not in control (all of which is ironic considering I am a pastor and the whole mystery of God thing). I got nervous; I got sick. The same thing happened in second grade when we were going to watch *Homeward Bound* in class, and I was terrified

---

1. The first part of this chapter talks about anxiety and related weight loss. If these are challenging topics for you, know that my freshman year and transition to college was challenging and skip to part 2 of this chapter.

that one of the animals was going to die. It happened on and off after that; it happened for a while after being in an eleven-car pile-up; when I freaked out when I first went overseas and realized how far away from home I was; when I had my first relationship (and subsequent ones for that matter); etc. And it happened when I went to college.

I started college off with band camp. I ended up loving marching with the Pride of Arizona marching band, but it was a little different than my high school marching band experience with sixty people. This was a 250-member ensemble, and band camp ran fourteen hours a day for a week, with a couple of breaks in there for lunch and dinner. It was August in Tucson, and I was drinking at least three of my two-liter camelback's worth of water every day and probably sweating most of it out. We worked hard. At meal times, as I got to know some of the other people in band, I struggled to eat more than half a sandwich, overcome with anxiety about all of these new things, about being away from my family, about making new friends, about being on my own, and probably about measuring up in the marching band that was kicking my butt. Knowing I needed to get protein into my body, my mom suggested getting smoothies with added protein powder, and thankfully, there was a place at U of A's union that had great smoothies! I didn't have to chew a smoothie, which helped. But by the time I went home for a visit three weeks after I had gone to school, I had lost some weight. I looked really skinny. As time passed and I adjusted enough to not experience so much anxiety, I was able to eat enough to at least maintain my weight, but then I got food poisoning later that year. Back home that summer, I was able to put it all back on thanks to my mom's familiar, good cooking and feeling more relaxed.

After those first few incredibly hard weeks, I started to adjust. My classes were fine, the people in marching band were nice, and I got involved with the Presbyterian Campus Ministry (PCM). I wasn't having the time of my life, though; far from it. I've never been a party person and am a pretty strong introvert, so figuring out a social life was hard. Being an introvert means that I recharge by being alone or with a small group of close friends, while being out in situations with a large group of strangers takes a lot of energy for me. For extroverts, being with lots of people provides energy, while being alone can be taxing. This all meant my inclination was not to go out after a long week. Plus, when I went to parties that one of my friends was at, for reasons I have never understood, she would call my ex and tell him to come, which led me to leave before he arrived to avoid that awkwardness.

The Best Four Years of Your Life?

My roommate and I got along well but were very different people. It was hard for me to find people I really felt like I connected with, and it was lonely. The only other freshman at PCM was a friend of mine from church back home who I would have dinner with every Tuesday before our PCM gathering. Some of the other students were nice, but they were pretty much all juniors and seniors with lots of memories of how things had been with the former campus minister. Overall, I was bored with my classes my first semester, which led me to take two upper-level religious studies courses my second semester, a decision that was good for me personally but was different from many of my peers. While I was fed by learning, they told me they wanted to take easy classes so they didn't have to spend as much time on them and had more free time for themselves to do whatever they wanted. It was for one of those upper-level religious studies classes that I first had Dr. Swaim and discovered a course that felt to me like what a college course was supposed to be—sitting in a circle discussing the deep, existential questions of life. The course was called Spirituality in the Arts, and that semester it was based on Jewish philosopher Martin Buber's work *I and Thou*, centering on relationships.

Looking back on my freshman year, there are a number of things I wish I could have told myself or wish I could have processed better in real time. First, getting help for my anxiety may have made my freshman year a little easier for me. It wouldn't have changed a lot of the pieces. I'm introverted even when I'm healthy, but it might have led to ways for me to feel more comfortable eating with others, and meals are often where freshman meet and get to know one another. Counseling centers work with plenty of students with anxiety these days. My advice would be that if something is having an impact on your well being, ask for help—check out your campus' counseling center if you have one. Being vulnerable and asking for help is being brave. Second, if college doesn't live up to what you hoped it would be right away (or ever), it's not your fault. I realized I felt guilt for having a rough freshman year and it shouldn't be that way. I got involved in stuff—marching band, a campus ministry, a leadership program—and it was still hard. College, and the transition to college, can just be hard for some of us. Finally, I can now name that some of what I felt was disappointment. Alongside what other people had told me to expect, I had built my own dreams of what college would be like, which for me really were around learning. I was excited for the classes I would have access to and what they would teach me. I was ready for higher learning! And as I sat in introductory courses to fill general education requirements, it was not all I hoped it would be. It's okay to be disappointed. It's okay to feel whatever it is you may be feeling. Things don't stop there.

Part 2: A Brief Look at the Next Three Years

I made it through freshman year. I got to know my campus minister really well, I made a few friends, and I started talking with Dr. Swaim. But it was far from the best year of my life. Sophomore year got better. It's nice to be a sophomore, and know what to expect from things, instead of feeling like you have no idea what's going on as a freshman. It also turned out that in both marching band and at PCM, many of the people who would be my closest friends were a year or two younger than me. Some new freshman came to PCM, and Shad, who was my age, transferred to U of A from a different college. Mike, who was a year older, also got re-involved in PCM. A new freshman in band and I connected, and I brought her to PCM with me. Lisa was from Phoenix, too, and we often carpooled to or from home together. I started to feel like these were people I could connect with, and indeed, they were. By second semester of sophomore year, I felt like I had a group of friends—people I wanted to be with, people who got me.

By the end of my sophomore year, life was good and had gotten better all throughout that second year. Two years is a long time, though. For me, it wasn't so much an issue of whether U of A was the right place for me, but for others it might be that transferring schools will help you find a better fit. In my case, it was about finding my place and my people, and it just took time. Even once I had found my place, there were still times when I would be overcome by a sense of loneliness, something that still occasionally happens for me. I think it's part of life. But the good moments started to far outweigh the bad ones, and that made my quality of life so much better.

As you start to feel more adjusted and like you have a good group of friends (and it's entirely normal for your friends to change, even more than once, while you're in college), it doesn't mean life won't present you with other challenges. In college, one of my closest friends found out that her parents were getting a divorce right around the start of her sophomore year. So much had changed for her in the past eighteen months, including her family moving from the Midwest to Arizona. Now, even her family was changing. It was incredibly hard and painful for her. One of the students I've worked with also had her parents go through a divorce right before she went to college. While college became this place she could escape, it made going home during breaks hard. Going home over her first Christmas break forced her to deal with emotions she had repressed without even realizing it. Another student's father went in for a medical procedure in October of his senior year of college. His father developed an infection, and due to some other pre-existing health issues, never recovered, passing away in December. While college can be a place to escape realities back home, it doesn't change the fact that things can happen and alter your college experience. Often, when your sense of home gets rattled, it takes a while to find solid footing again, and hopefully you will have others to lean on to help get you through this time. Don't forget that your school probably also gives you access to counseling, which can be helpful for anyone at any point in life, even when things are going well!

This leads us to the Scripture at the beginning of this chapter. There are many things I love about Psalms, including that it is the prayer book of the Bible. In its pages and prayers, you can find just about every emotion. There is joy and happiness, sadness and fear, depression and loneliness, anger and fury; it's all there. I love how the psalmists just put it out there, praise of God along with hard and painful questions for God, including wondering if God is even there. Most psalms start with the tough stuff, but then have a turning point in them, a transition. As in Ps 86, there is a switch from supplication to praise. This mirrors many of the experiences I have had in life, including college. Things can have a rough start. We can wonder where God is, if God is present at times we feel so incredibly alone. I'll wonder if I can do it, but then often reach a point where I realize, after some deep breaths and probably a few phone calls or conversations, "Ok, I think I've got this, and more importantly, God's got me." Hopefully, I then remember to offer up my praise and thanksgiving like the psalmists as well. We may take some more steps backward and forward, but God is always with us on the journey. Psalms reflects our own prayers in many ways.

As you continue through college, suddenly three years have passed and you are down to the final one. My senior year was an emotional roller coaster, which I think is not an uncommon experience. On the one hand, you've gotten this college thing pretty well figured out. Now that you're a senior, you get to be one of the leaders in the things you're involved in if you want to be. You also might get a little more recognition for the work you put into things. I kept a journal for my thesis during my senior year, and that December I wrote, "It feels good to know that I am passionate about what I do, and to have that recognized by others. . . . I think that as a senior, I felt more confident to begin with, and meeting with success has increased this. . . . As a senior this year, I feel people do acknowledge what you have done more, and it feels kind of awesome to be seen as great." I wrote this reflecting on a quote by Marianne Williamson (which you can read in full in the "Conclusion") that asks, "Who am I to be brilliant, gorgeous, talented, and fabulous? Actually, who are you *not* to be?"[2] It says that as children of God, we were meant to shine, and while what I wrote in my journal sounds somewhat conceited at first glance, it was more about feeling like I was finally really allowing myself to shine, and that felt great. I was leading a book discussion for PCM on Rob Bell's *Velvet Elvis*, I had received a game ball for marching band that fall (a smaller football given after each game to someone who had worked especially hard that week), and over Christmas break I began the process to become an ordained minister and received a tremendous amount of support.

So on the one hand, I was shining, living into who God had created me to be. I also had been struggling with having lots of questions and doubts (as I share more about in chapter five), and while still wanting to go to seminary was wondering if I would actually make a good pastor. Then, there was the reality that this was all going to be over before I knew it, and I was looking at moving across the country, far away from the wonderful friends who now felt like family to me. Most of my friends weren't graduating yet, and this made my leaving harder for them. Knowing it was all about to be over made me sad, really sad. It also made me want to get the most out of the time I had left with them. I was terrified and excited about what was coming next.

College is a journey. For many of us, it's a journey from youth to young adulthood. It's a time of self-exploration and discovery, of finding and building your own community, and it can be a roller-coaster ride. Like a roller coaster, it can scare the hell out of us, and it can be exciting and fun. I am grateful for my college experience, but I wouldn't call it the best four years of my life, and it's A-OK if that's not true for you either. In fact, hopefully you'll find a lot more to love after college, too.

PRAYER

Eternal God,
This college experience is a wild ride,

---

2. Williamson, *Return to Love*, 190–91.

With deep valleys and mountaintops,
With moments of triumph and moments of despair.
Help us to know that each of our experiences is valid,
That there is not a right or a wrong,
That there is no "expected" experience we have to accomplish,
And that it is good to ask for help when we need it.
Remind us that we are not alone,
That others have gone through this before us,
And that you are always holding us close.
Help us find people who we can share with,
Who we can talk to about how we are really doing,
The friends who will be there through thick and thin.
Guide us to those relationships,
And to the mentors who will enrich our lives,
That we may live into who you created us to be.
Amen.

Reflection Questions

1. What has your college experience been like? Where are you at on the journey now?
2. How has college been what you expected? How has it been different from what you expected?
3. Did you have people tell you that college would be the best four years of your life? What did this make you think? What do you think about that phrase now?

2

Finding a Space to Be Your True Self and Embrace All That You Are

> Sexy is when you love being you.
>
> —Rob Bell

> To be beautiful means to be yourself. You don't need to be accepted by others. You need to accept yourself. When you are born a lotus flower, be a beautiful lotus flower, don't try to be a magnolia flower. If you crave acceptance and recognition and try to change yourself to fit what other people want you to be, you will suffer all your life. True happiness and true power lie in understanding yourself, accepting yourself, having confidence in yourself.
>
> —Thich Nhat Hanh

Scripture

> O Lord, you have searched me and known me.
> You know when I sit down and when I rise up;
> you discern my thoughts from far away.
> You search out my path and my lying down,
> and are acquainted with all my ways.
> Even before a word is on my tongue,
> O Lord, you know it completely.
> You hem me in, behind and before,
> and lay your hand upon me.
> Such knowledge is too wonderful for me;

Finding a Space to Be Your True Self

it is so high that I cannot attain it.
Where can I go from your spirit?
Or where can I flee from your presence?
If I ascend to heaven, you are there;
if I make my bed in Sheol, you are there.
If I take the wings of the morning
and settle at the farthest limits of the sea,
even there your hand shall lead me,
and your right hand shall hold me fast.
If I say, "Surely the darkness shall cover me,
and the light around me become night,"
even the darkness is not dark to you;
the night is as bright as the day,
for darkness is as light to you.
For it was you who formed my inward parts;
you knit me together in my mother's womb.
I praise you, for I am fearfully and wonderfully made.
(Ps 139:1–14a)

I ABSOLUTELY LOVE THE QUOTE from Rob Bell above. It's actually not something he said; it's something his wife Kristen (not the actress) said, when their four-year-old son came home from preschool one day and asked them what the word "sexy" means. When we hear that question, many of us probably think it means many things that we don't believe we are. We think of fashionable, expensive clothing that perfectly fits a sculpted body. We think of *People Magazine's* "Sexiest Man Alive" issue or *Sports Illustrated's* "Swimsuit" edition, or for that matter any *Sports Illustrated* featuring shirtless male athletes with perfect abs. We think of influencers, movie stars, and superheroes, expensive cars, and money. We think of what our culture has taught us to believe "sexy" is without stopping to question if we would actually even find that appealing.

When I stop to think about moments when I love being me, it's when I feel like my best and most authentic self, when I feel like I am the child of God I was created to be. Kristen Bell was answering her four-year-old, and so her answer seems to be about what attracts us, what draws us, to others, both romantically and platonically. People who embrace who they are inherently make us want to spend time with or be around that person, including family, friends, and mentors. When I watch other people love being themselves in a moment, there is no way to deny how incredibly attractive that is in a person. It's a chance to see who they were meant to be, to watch them shine. In these moments, you see a contentment, a joy, a sense of fulfillment that bubbles up within a person and just overflows. They sparkle and can't help it. Their talents are being utilized and life itself seems to be a gift. The joy is contagious. When I am in the presence of someone who clearly just loves being themselves, it makes me feel brighter, too. When I love being me, I'm less self-conscious and more willing to be goofy and just have fun, because I am a child of God and it doesn't matter if my dance moves are not quite up to par (believe me, they aren't). I'm in a space that allows me to safely be more vulnerable.

Part of transitioning to adulthood is about finding and creating the space for these moments to happen, about finding spaces to belong. Growing up, I had two different groups of friends. One group was my friends from church. I met my three closest friends at church between the ages of two and four; we had basically known each other our entire lives, or at least as long as we could remember. We were fairly uninhibited together. We were really good friends who could laugh at and with one another, around whom we knew it was okay to be goofy, but unless we planned to get together outside of church activities, they were friends who I saw only once or twice a week. The people I saw everyday were my school friends, since my sister and I were pretty much the only ones from our church who went to our school. In high school, I had a number of close friends at school, many of whom were also in marching band. I liked these friends and had good relationships with them. Still, being a high school student who wants to go to seminary has its challenges. None of my friends at school actively practiced any religion, and with my faith being so central to my identity, at times I felt they didn't really get an essential part of me. We could hang out, we could talk about life, but it felt like they didn't understand something that was at the core of my being. Much of the time it didn't seem like this mattered, until those moments when it felt like it truly did in sometimes painful ways.

College was a place where I was able to find a space where I felt totally accepted and understood, though it took some time. I found a group of people who seemed to understand all of who I was and were my friends because of it. As these friendships developed, some of them led to being housemates as well. At college, it seems that almost no matter what your interests or passions might be, there is a space for you to pursue them or find others with common interests. By my senior year, I had figured this

Finding a Space to Be Your True Self

out, writing in my thesis journal that December, "College is the place where it does not matter who you are; you can find your niche and if you want, really shine."[1] When you go on a college tour, the guide often brags about the number of clubs or activities that you can get involved in at that school. With so many different groups, you can find one that interests you, and often within that group, find the people who you connect with really well. These can become the spaces where you feel that you can just be who you are, as a person and in that moment, and know that you will be loved and accepted. Finding these spaces is essential for our well-being. Too much of the time, we feel like we have to wear a mask to hide what we are truly feeling, or even who we really are. While there are times and places where this can be helpful, and maybe safest, we also need spaces where the mask can come off and we can be our true selves, full of strength and vulnerability.

When you feel comfortable living with a group of people, you can just be you, quirks and all. In my case, this meant my senior-year housemates—Cassie, Mike, and Shad—perceived my true self to at times be more of a grandma than a twenty-one-year-old. And my friends laughed at me for it and loved me for it. One night, Cassie came downstairs to find me on the couch watching TV and said, "Megan, you are like the epitome of an old grandma right now. Do you realize that?" To be fair, she had a point. I was probably watching something older people might have also enjoyed, maybe *The West Wing*. But I wasn't just watching TV, I was knitting while I did so and had curlers in my hair, the sponge ones that you put in while your hair is wet and sleep in so that in the morning when your hair is dry you take them out and ideally have nice curls. I, in all of my grandmotherliness, was perfectly content and happy. We had so much fun together that year, though at times we drove each other crazy. We learned to have discussions about not leaving dishes in the sink and sharing the cooking and cleanup. When Cassie and I returned from an international trip to a stairwell lined with beer bottles that made it difficult to get our suitcases up the stairs for fear of shattered glass, we found it far less funny than Mike and Shad, who were proud of their accomplishment. There are so many more good memories though, which made the bumps in the road totally worth it. There are days when I miss them all, and times when I'm nostalgic and wish I could be back in that time and place. It wasn't perfect, but we loved and accepted each other.

---

1. I kept a journal during my final year of college as I researched and wrote my senior thesis. I'll be quoting from it throughout the book.

You're Not the Only One

There were other parts of my college experience, such as extracurriculars, that played a part in helping me embrace all of myself as well, experiences God used to help me grow and discover who I am. This has been true for many of the students I have worked with, who have joined groups ranging from ballroom dance and theater to robotics or aerospace engineering clubs to a club for playing games like "Mafia." Many have also joined groups where they can connect with people with similar identities. For me, being in the marching band was a huge part of my time at college. I didn't do a lot of socializing with many people from band outside of band stuff, but being a part of the Pride of Arizona throughout my four years allowed me to be a part of something much bigger than myself, pushed me to work harder and be better, and kept me playing music, something that is an essential part of me. I was a part of a leadership program my freshman and sophomore years as well, which I enjoyed, but then decided there were other things in which I would rather invest my time. Classes can also be a part of this. I needed classes that challenged me, which led me to jump into a couple of upper-level classes my second semester of freshman year. They were both great! One of them was my first class with Dr. Swaim and was a class where we were pushed to be vulnerable and authentic. PCM had a big role to play beyond the friendships I formed there. Pastor Ben provided a place where I was able to test out my call to ministry. When I asked about a book study, he told me I should lead it. Ben gave me the opportunity to lead several different groups, and I learned more about how to be a leader and affirmed that this was the type of thing I liked doing in the process. All of these things played a part in helping me discover and live into my true self, the person God created me to be, a person I am always continuing to get to know, who keeps growing and changing. How are you working to get to know your true self?

Psalm 139 is a beautiful psalm because it reminds us we have been fearfully and wonderfully made by God. Yes, I, too, get a little caught up in the whole science versus role of God here and what it means that God knit us in our mother's womb. I know things like my appearance and many of my personality traits can be explained scientifically, and I still believe God was involved in creating me to be who I am as a person. God has a part in creating and shaping us, helping us realize and live into the child of God we are intended to be, the person who will make us feel the most alive when we are that person. God is a part of our nature and our nurture, which work together to make us into who we are and are becoming. It's important to realize that our true selves exist now, but that it also isn't static, and as we grow in maturity and in discipleship, we may change. We must find a way to have compassionate introspection of our own lives, seeing ways we can continue to grow and improve, but also sitting in God's grace as we do so and knowing God loves us as we currently are.

The truth is that God knows us intimately. It is likely that God does actually know us better than we know our own self, or better than we allow ourselves to know our own self. Inward journeys are hard, and many of us seem to try to avoid them. Our true self also has pain and hurt. This can be some of the hardest stuff not just to allow others to see, but to actually admit exists to ourselves. It can feel easier to just create a nice appearance, one that we think people will like, than to be us, with our wounds and sometimes grumpy moods. God wants to be in the midst of that pain, and letting God in may help us to allow others to see us in our vulnerability as well. God became human in Jesus, a vulnerable baby who lived a life in which there was joy, pain, and sadness, so that we could understand that God wants to share life with us in a very real way, in every aspect of life.

Many of us struggle to truly believe that God wants to be with us in the midst of the good and the messy, that God will truly love and claim us, warts and all. Sometimes, it may even feel safest to run away or to hide, but there is absolutely nowhere—nowhere—that we can go where God is not already present. The passage is not just talking about physical locations either, even though that is the language it is using. It tells us that in our best moments, the moments we feel like we are on top of the world and on fire, God is there. In our worst moments, the moments when we don't want to even get out of bed or are laying on the floor sobbing and feeling like a total mess, the moments we feel completely broken and are not sure how to continue, God is there. God is there, even when we don't want God to be there. The psalmist says that such knowledge is too wonderful to grasp, and indeed, it can seem hard to believe that the God of the universe cares about each of us so powerfully. That's pretty incredible and hopefully makes you realize how unbelievably much God loves you.

The truth is, such knowledge *is* too wonderful to grasp. In my thesis journal, as I began my final semester of college, I wrote, "I am who I am, and I am okay with that. I am learning to be who God made me to be." Part of what I like about what I wrote is that it is real. I wrote that I was "okay" with that because a lot of the time, especially during parts of college, I would say that "okay" described how I felt about myself. There are plenty of times when I didn't, and still don't, love being me. I'm not always willing to stop and remember that I am fearfully and wonderfully made and to praise God for that. I am indeed still learning how to be the person who God made me to be. I make mistakes. I do things that immediately feel wrong. I spend way to much time questioning something that I said or did, wondering how it might have been perceived, hoping that I didn't accidentally offend someone, or replaying old offenses with guilt. In all of this, God is present with me, claiming me still, just as God claims you.

When we find spaces where we feel free to be our true selves, without any kind of mask, we are in places or with people who serve as reminders of God's love for us, who can offer us a glimpse of what God's love is like and see the ways in which God has provided opportunities for us to grow. Throughout my life, it has been faith communities where I have felt this most powerfully. A few years ago, wanting to update the existing description of the CA, the student board came up with a new one: "The CA is a student community where all are invited to explore their faith and question what they believe, and are welcomed to be whoever the heck they are!" We need these places in our lives! In the moments where we love being exactly who we are, we experience what God wants for us, an experience of joy and fulfillment that draws others in. In these moments you experience the beauty of knowing that you have been fearfully and wonderfully made, and help others to know that they are, too.

Prayer

Overwhelming God,
You have searched us,
And know us,
Better than we are willing to know ourselves.
Help us to live into the people
You have created us to be.
Lead us to people and places
Where we find love and acceptance,
A place to be our true selves,
And know our gifts and our shortcomings
Will all be accepted.
Thank you for how experiences of belonging
Show us reflections of your love,
A love too strong for us to grasp.

Finding a Space to Be Your True Self

Remind us you have claimed us,
That you have shaped us,
And help us allow you to help us love who we are,
To find the joy of living as a child of God,
And in doing so share this joy with all those around us.
Amen.

Reflection Questions

1. What do you think of how Kristen Bell defined "sexy"? Are there times when you love being you? What do those times feel like? What does it feel like to watch others do the same?

2. What holds you back from being your true self? Knowing that there are times and places where it is best to protect ourselves, do you still hold back more often than you might need to? What might you do to change this? How might that impact you?

3. How would you describe your true self? Where have you found spaces in which it is safe to be your true self? What has made it that way? Why is it important to have times when we are able to freely be ourselves?

4. Do you feel like you can somewhat understand how much God loves you, or is such "knowledge too wonderful . . . to attain?" (Ps 139:6). Who or what represents God's love in your own life?

3

Learning to Be True to Yourself, and That It's Okay to Have Water in Your Red Solo Cup

> We take long trips.
> We puzzle over the meaning of a painting or a book,
> when what we're wanting to see and understand
> in this world, we are that.
>
> —Rumi

> The only tyrant I accept in this world is the "still small voice" within me. And even though I have to face the prospect of being a minority of one, I humbly believe I have the courage to be in such a hopeless minority.
>
> —Mahatma Gandhi

Scripture

The proverbs of Solomon son of David, king of Israel:
For learning about wisdom and instruction,
for understanding words of insight,
for gaining instruction in wise dealing,
righteousness, justice, and equity;
to teach shrewdness to the simple,
knowledge and prudence to the young—
let the wise also hear and gain in learning,
and the discerning acquire skill,
to understand a proverb and a figure,

the words of the wise and their riddles.
The fear of the Lord is the beginning of knowledge;
fools despise wisdom and instruction.
Hear, my child, your father's instruction,
and do not reject your mother's teaching;
for they are a fair garland for your head,
and pendants for your neck.
(Prov 1:1–9)

Train children in the right way,
and when old, they will not stray.
(Prov 22:6)

IN MY OPINION, THERE are way too many movies that portray college as this wild and crazy place, where everyone is in a sorority or fraternity and does nothing but drink and act crazy and stupid all the time, spending a good chunk of their time in or near a pool. They also manage to not end up facing any serious consequences for the decisions they make. You've probably seen some of these, though if I'm being honest, I've seen more trailers than the movies themselves because whether they are a parody or a straight-up comedy; the genre is not my cup of tea. While this is not the actual reality of college for the majority of students, even most of those who are in Greek life, these movies are part of the cultural machine that can influence what we think we are supposed to do and who we should be when we go to college. In most media portrayals, the student who focuses on academic work is pictured as never having any fun, being unfashionable, and living in the library. There are also stories about extracurriculars, like a capella groups or sports teams, but they tend to focus solely on that part of the experience and not show the rest of the character's college life (though they often still show the parties and drinking). Rarely do we get healthy, good depictions of a college student with a well-rounded life, probably because it would just feel normal and not all that exciting. Regardless of whether it's Hollywood material or not, this regular, well-functioning life is what most students should anticipate trying to create for themselves during their time at college.

One of the things about myself that I've known and accepted is that I've never had the desire to get wasted, for a variety of reasons. While this is not how many of my peers in undergrad behaved, it was what felt best for me personally, what I felt comfortable with. I don't assume this is necessarily true for you, nor do I think it needs to be, but I also know it may be how you feel, too. It took some work and time to figure out exactly how I wanted to engage with some of these social scenes on campus. I don't remember if I worried about being seen as uncool or not, but I also knew I didn't want to do something that felt like selling myself out. And until I was about twenty-one, I didn't like the taste of alcohol, so why would I want to drink something that tasted gross? Ultimately, I still would go to parties in college because I wanted to hang out with friends. Sometimes I would go as the DD (designated driver), which makes it really easy to not be drinking or to limit your drinking. Your friends, if they are good friends, tend to want people to get home safely, and if you are the one responsible for that, that's totally cool. They often were glad to have someone volunteer to drive, and when we stopped by the store for them to get alcohol, I got a box of Frosted Mini-Wheats to enjoy. Other times, I didn't trust what was being served, some type of jungle juice with who-knew-what in it. In those circumstances, I would get a red Solo cup, find the kitchen, and fill it with water. To everyone there, I had a cup in hand and was having a good time. It also allowed me to be a part of the festivities in a way that felt safe and enjoyable for me. Playing a drinking game one night, I refilled my empty beer bottle with water. When the guy I was sitting next to somehow found out, he said something like, "That's a smart idea." He didn't think I was uncool or make fun of me for it, he thought what I was doing made a lot of sense. Still, I can't say every choice I made along the way was the right one, that I didn't wrestle with it, or that I always made choices for the right reasons; it was all a part of my continuing to grow up.

You're going to change at college, growing from the person you have been into the person you are becoming. You would change even if you didn't go to college, if you never left home and took a job at the coffee shop down the road, or if you went to community college, or joined the military. Change is part of growing up. Despite my still having days when I just want to be a kid again, I know that actually being a kid is in my past (breaking out and playing our old Super Nintendo is still fun though—it's practically an antique!). It's true you could change for better or for worse, but most of the time it will be for the better. You will change because now things are up to you, and not just figuring out how to make your dirty laundry clean and if you want to get up for that early-morning class. What you choose to believe, what you consider right and wrong, what you are going to do with your newfound freedom—it's all up to you now. You have both the opportunity and the responsibility of making decisions for yourself and of making sure not to lose yourself in the midst of it all.

For most chapters in this book, I've tried to pair the chapter with a passage of Scripture that we can reflect on in relationship to the topic at hand, that might offer some wisdom. In this chapter, I find that the quotes offer the wisdom, and the Scripture offers the set-up. The book of Proverbs is part of what is called the wisdom literature of the Bible. In part, Proverbs is about handing down wisdom from one generation to the next, about teaching children how to lead a righteous life. When we hear something from Proverbs, we often hear snippets, a verse or two, which is due to the nature of the book.

What Proverbs reveals to us, however, is that there has long been a biblical tradition of teaching children how to live a faithful life. From the time we were little, hopefully most of us had people—parents, teachers, coaches, or others—helping us learn what was right and wrong, how we should behave, and what was good or bad. These people tended to enforce consequences when we made the wrong choice, be that stealing a cookie before dinner, coming home after curfew, or deciding not to do some assignment or ditch a class, and these consequences were often enforced whether or not we agreed with what they said and whether or not the consequences were the right response. When we go to college, we will take what these adults in our lives have taught us along with us. Just as the book of Proverbs is about handing down wisdom, the adults in our lives send us with a collection of "Proverbs" to take with us as we go on to the next stage in life. They go alongside the lessons we have learned ourselves along the way, sometimes through our own trial and error.

Though many of us go to college with a strong sense of right and wrong, sometimes we have yet to put a lot of thought into why things may fall into the category they do. Some of us will go to college having put little conscious thought into our ethics or our moral principles, period. The reality is, whether you have thought much about it or not, there is a voice inside all of us, a gut sense of what is right and wrong, a conscience.[1] Until now, you may have had people telling you what to decide, and sometimes, you'll be tempted to grab your cell phone and call them up to ask them to decide for you. It's not bad to seek guidance in life, especially on major decisions, but you're at a point where you are ready to have more responsibility and to

---

1. Shel Silverstein's poem "The Voice" captures this well. You can find it in Silverstein, *Falling Up*, 38.

make more decisions for yourself. Listen to that inner voice, the voice that comes from who you are, all you have been taught over the years, who you believe God wants you to be, and even who you hope to someday be. There may be times you experience pressure from friends or even a significant other to do something the voice is cautioning you against, so as the Blue Fairy tells Pinocchio, "Always let your conscience be your guide."[2] It's there for a reason and may even be the Holy Spirit offering some guidance. Also know that God's love and grace abound, and nothing you have done or will do could stop God from loving you (though you may still have earthly consequences to face).

I pair this with the Rumi quote because so often we feel like we make decisions in pursuit of something, be it freedom, happiness, meaning, or even oblivion. Rumi invites us to look inside ourselves to find whatever it is we spend our lives chasing after, the answer we are trying to find. Rumi invites us to know ourselves in a way that can be challenging because it can push us past what feels comfortable, but it helps us to truly know ourselves and to be able to hear and listen to our inner voice.

All this being said, college can be a time when we test some things out as well, to see if they feel right or wrong, and it's likely both will happen. It's okay for you to decide you think something is okay even if you used to believe it was not, as long as it's for the right reasons, which means not just because your friends want you to do it. There are definitely things many of our parents taught us that they could not honestly say they themselves followed. Sometimes they want to try to keep us from the pain and damage of the mistakes they made, other times they are overly protective. College is supposed to be a time when we take all that we were taught up until this point and make it our own, and sometimes this does look like understanding something in a different way than you previously had. My own opinions changed about a number of things while I was at college, some of which I discovered I had no idea where they came from but had somehow creeped into my ideology over time. I realized there were things I felt were the proper Christian belief, only to realize over time that life was not nearly that black and white, neither was the Bible, and that having a strong moral compass is really important as your beliefs change and expand.

I say all of this not to sound like I'm preaching or like I am telling you what is right and what is wrong or being judgmental. I say this because I have seen too many students make a decision in the moment without

---

2. Sharpsteen et al., *Pinocchio*, 18:32.

having thought through what feels right for them, only to feel like they betrayed themselves later on. I also say this because I wish someone had told me it's not just okay, but it's normal to decide not to do "what everyone else is doing." Sure, people told me it was okay, but I wish someone had told me there were others not drinking, showed me the stats on how the majority of college students are not hooking up with random partners, and told me there were others looking for meaningful friendships and relationships, so that being true to myself didn't always feel so lonely.

What does being true to yourself look like? It looks like not losing yourself, who you are, what you want for yourself, what feels good and what makes you feel anxious, in the midst of the vast number of new experiences you may be exposed to. It means owning the things you are passionate about and sharing the things that give you great joy with those close to you. It means finding someone with whom you can share that you feel confused and lost if, at the beginning of senior year, you feel like you chose the wrong major and have no idea what you want to do with your life anymore. It can mean being open to exploring your sexual or gender identity. It also means thinking about what boundaries you want for yourself around drugs, alcohol, and sexual behavior, and ideally before you find yourself in a situation where you are forced to make a decision under pressure. It means knowing that you may choose differently than you had expected in the moment.

Being true to yourself is also essential when it comes to romantic relationships. College is a time when a lot of young people experience a lot of firsts, possibly including your first serious relationship. This has been true for a number of the students that I have worked with at the CA. Again, pop culture as well as university culture can make it easy to believe that there are certain ways and behaviors that are expected of you in a relationship, and it's important to remember that even if people are saying "everyone" is doing something, that is probably not at all the case. The percentage may be far lower than you imagine. One evening at the CA a few years back, I was sitting and talking with three students, Jess, Lauren, and Conner. As often happens in conversations with students, at some point the topic of conversation became relationships. Lauren, a sophomore, had very recently started casually dating a guy who attended a school nearby. She didn't have a lot of prior dating experience, while the guy she was seeing had significantly more experience. Mostly the students were talking, and I was listening to them, when she asked, "How long can you date someone before it's unfair not to have sex with them?" Her language took all three of us by surprise. I think we expected her to be thinking about if she felt ready and wanted this for herself. "Unfair" signified that this was about the pressures being put on her by her partner and what she felt she owed him.

One of the joys of my work is watching students grow into these wonderful young adults, and in the conversation occurring that night, Conner, the only guy in the room, was amazing. Conner was in a long-term relationship with a young woman he had been dating for about a year and a half. Both he and Jess immediately picked up on the word "unfair," and the idea that at some point you "owe" sex to your partner. Both were quick to say that this was not an issue of fairness. Lauren said that the guy she was seeing was making her feel bad that she didn't feel ready to have sex with him, and this was after about three weeks of kind-of dating. Conner asked Lauren several good questions and affirmed that, first and foremost, we were talking about her body and that she needed to feel comfortable and want to have sex with the guy before doing so. Conner also was clear that being in a good relationship means your partner should respect where you are at. He talked about growing together and progressing gradually at a pace that both partners felt comfortable with. Conner helped not only with good advice for this specific situation, but in also assuring both of these young women that they were smart, beautiful, and should never sell themselves short when it came to romantic partners or compromise their self-worth for someone else. My heart felt so full watching him do this.

Learning exactly what your values are and what it means to live them out is a process, and there is no "right" way to do it. To some extent, it will often be a bit messy and complicated. Sometimes compromising on core values will have a big impact on you. Other times, you might have to make compromises along the way that don't feel as tied to your sense of self and self-worth, such as keeping a work-study job you might not love but need the income from. There is also a possibility you might worry you're missing out if you chose to skip something that didn't feel right for you. It's okay to feel this way and doesn't mean you made the wrong decision. This kind of understanding our values and our priorities is something you will continue to do for the rest of your life.

Whatever you do, try to listen to that inner voice, that one that is grounded in what you have been taught over the course of your life and anchors you in what is right for you. Make your faith a part of that grounding. Form a relationship with a pastor or adult who can help you dig into Scripture and look at how a text that is thousands of years old can apply to our lives today (don't worry—it's really not just a bunch of prohibitions! We know Jesus changed water into wine to keep the party going). Spend time in prayer. Know that God extends forgiveness to us, wants us to learn from our mistakes, and to also forgive ourselves when we make choices we aren't proud of. Let God's grace surround you and help you live into who you were created to be.

Prayer

God of grace,
We thank you for who you created us to be,
With the many things we love about ourselves,
And the pieces of us we struggle to accept;
All of which comprise our identity.
As we journey through these college years,
Help us to be true to ourselves,
To listen to the voice deep within us,
That contains the wisdom of those who love us,
Through which your Spirit speaks to us.
Help us to accept responsibility for our own life and choices,
To know that we have to make decisions for ourselves.
Lead us to relationships in which we can be open and honest,
Sharing our joys and fears,
Trusting that these friends and mentors won't "dump" us
When we show the person behind the mask,
But support us on the journey,
And share themselves with us.
Forgive us when we make decisions that hurt ourselves or others,
When we do not listen to your guidance.
Allow us to experience your grace,
And not live lives weighed down by guilt.
Help us be the children of God you created us to be.
Amen.

Reflection Questions

1. Where have your ideas of what is right and wrong come from? Were there life lessons you learned growing up that you think are important

to adhere to as you become an adult? How do you decide if something is right or wrong when the decision is up to you?

2. Do you feel like you are often true to yourself, or do you feel like you are prone to give in to what you think others expect of you, even when it feels wrong? How do you feel about this? What role do you think social media plays, along with entertainment culture, in influencing the decisions that you make?

3. Do you think the Bible provides guidance on how we decide if things are right or wrong? How do we get wisdom from a book that is two thousand–plus years old? What does it mean for the Bible to be a living text, and where else might we also look for God's guidance?

4

There's No Place Like Home

> Is this home? Is this where I should learn to be happy? . . .
> I was told, every day in my childhood, Even when we grow old.
> Home will be where the heart is. Never were words so true.
> My heart's far, far, away. Home is too.
>
> —"Home," *Beauty and the Beast*

> More and more of us are rooted in the future or the present tense as much as in the past. And home, we know, is not just the place where you happen to be born. It's the place where you become yourself.
>
> —Pico Iyer

Scripture

> Everyone then who hears these words of mine and acts on them will be like a wise man who built his house on rock. The rain fell, the floods came, and the winds blew and beat on that house, but it did not fall, because it had been founded on rock. And everyone who hears these words of mine and does not act on them will be like a foolish man who built his house on sand. The rain fell, and the floods came, and the winds blew and beat against that house, and it fell—and great was its fall! (Matt 7:24–27)

I WAS BORN IN KANSAS, and so my family has always made "Oz" references. As I was getting ready to leave for school, my mom and I were out shopping one day, and found these *The Wizard of Oz* pajama pants. One pair had little cartoons of the Lion, Scarecrow, and Tin Man on them, with the words "heartless," "spineless," and "brainless," respectively, beneath them, and then said something about it being hard to find a good man. Then, there was a pair with black fabric, little white stick houses, and the phrase "There's no place like home" printed all over them. We thought that those would be good pajama pants to have to take to college.

Moving to college was a hard experience for me.[1] I had lived in the same house for basically my entire life. My parents moved into the house when I was one, and my younger sister was brought home from the hospital to this house when she was born about eighteen months later. Some people move around a lot while they are growing up, others share their time between two houses; I lived in only one that I can remember. My parents lived there until I was twenty-five years old. To me, that house meant home, and it was a good home. Some of you will have wanted out of your house as soon as possible for a whole variety of reasons, but I was a homebody in a very stable, loving, and trusting household. All of this meant I had put a lot of value on our physical home. I still remember listening to the conversation my parents were having one night while I was in high school. I was sitting doing homework at the kitchen counter and they were standing in the kitchen, so really, it would have been hard for me to not listen as there was only about seven feet between us. We had lived in this house since I was one year old, and my parents were now talking about if they wanted to look at selling our house and moving into a different one. It was not because of moving for a new job or anything like that; in my mind it was just because. The idea made me furious! Why would we sell our home? Nostrils flaring, I burst out in anger. My parents laughed—apparently, I resembled my mother at a younger age and they found this humorous. I did not find the concept of them getting rid of our home to be humorous at all, neither did I appreciate them laughing at me. My parents, both having grown up in one house as well, knew that our house was important to me and my sister and that it represented much more than just a house. They also knew that "home" was not just about the space but about the people, and that had we moved, a different space could also have felt like home.

---

1. I had an ideal home environment growing up. I don't take that for granted. I know for many young people this is not the case, and that for some, leaving their childhood home also means freedom from a toxic environment. If that is your story, then getting to develop a new home may be the first time you get to experience what "home" can really mean for you.

There's No Place Like Home

Having lived in the same home throughout my childhood, moving away to school felt weird. While I made my dorm room my own space, I'm not sure it ever really felt like home to me. Sure, I put up a three-by-four-foot poster on the wall with pictures from back home and inspirational quotes, I picked out a bed spread, and had a few knickknacks, but I found it hard to make an institutional, shared shoebox feel like home. I grew up with my own bedroom, which was also a place to go and be alone when needed. Now, it was hard for half of a not-very-large dorm room, with my roommate's stuff scattered about (thankfully on her half) and very limited privacy, to really feel like my own space. When my sister had something on the TV that I found annoying, I could walk to the next room. When my roommate did, I'd have to put headphones in and turn music up loud enough not to hear it or leave the building in search of somewhere to go (there was not a good study lounge in my dorm).

Life in a dorm was a major adjustment. Back home, no one ran up and down the halls screaming at three a.m. like my new hall mates did some nights. My roommate and I got along, but I was now living with someone who was basically a stranger, and we were very different from each other. My family all kept relatively similar hours, but my new roommate and I did not. She would call her boyfriend about the time I went to bed, and be on the phone for hours (she was nice and went into the hall). She often would just be getting up when I had returned from my day's first activity. Not only do you and this other person live in a small room, you might be sharing a bathroom with twenty other people, one that doesn't get cleaned on the weekends when it often needs to be cleaned the most! There's a song that still brings back bad memories because one of my hall mates had it playing, seemingly on repeat, in the bathroom while I was in there sick with food poisoning (and yes, it really was food poisoning—if the chicken nuggets in your dorm freezer seem suspicious and are bendable, then my advice is don't eat them). I'm a person who likes musicals, and on my more dramatic days, I probably found myself feeling like Belle, having arrived at the castle only to find it not what she'd hoped. My heart and home felt far away, too. It probably didn't help that I was the oldest sibling, so home hadn't been changed yet the way it is for younger siblings when the older siblings go away to school or move out to find a place of their own.

In many ways, I had even less to process in my transition than others will. Overall, I had a lot less culture shock to deal with than many will experience when they go to college. Sure, there was the shock of moving away from my family and home and now being on my own, but I went to a school about two hours away and one in a very similar climate to the one I was coming from. Some of you will have moved much farther away and possibly to a place that feels like an alien world. Be it going from living in a rural area to college in a metropolitan area, or from growing up in a city and moving to a university that feels like it's in the middle of nowhere, location can really throw us. As can the weather. I moved from Arizona to New Jersey for grad school, and during my first year there I called my mom in early March asking where spring was. She just laughed and said I had a good month or more to wait yet. This was not cool with me. In the desert, spring was mid-February. Moving to a place with a climate that is different than what you are used to is a major adjustment. It's amazing the number of students at Penn I work with who come without a good winter coat and think they can get away without one, only to realize that it really does help to have one as Philadelphia can be very cold in the winter. There are also some of you who will be international students and really feel like you are far, far away from home, in a culture that may feel (and be) completely foreign to you.

Know that whether you are across the world or country, or even at a school in your hometown, feeling homesick is normal. Give yourself grace as you adjust to living in a new place. Seek out help if you feel especially blue—things like SAD (seasonal affective disorder—feeling depressed during winter months) are real and affect more people than you might think. Also, while you can talk to people on the phone or via the internet, one of the things you may find you miss most about home are your pets. It's not just them that we miss, but what they provide for us. A pet can be a friend that comes and curls up or snuggles with us, who gets excited to see us when we get home, and if they are like the three dogs I've had in my life, loves to give kisses. Losing this at a time when we may lose most of the physical touch we have in our lives can affect our wellbeing. Don't be afraid to go up to someone who has a dog on campus and ask if you can pet the dog—just make sure to ask first! You can also find a shelter near your school to go volunteer at. It's helpful to be able to name and acknowledge what we miss, and to think about where we may seek it out.

In many ways, like Dorothy and the pajama pants said, there really is "no place like home." I used to think home was a place, and in some ways it is. If I were to go back to the house I grew up in today, even though it now has different people's stuff in it, I imagine that it would have a feeling of familiarity to it, that it would feel like home. I could walk around the house in the dark and know the layout of the rooms. Unless they have been changed, I would find the quirks of the house familiar—the pantry door that sticks when you try to close it, the landscaping, the color of the paint. I would remember many happy years in that space. But I also know that home is more than just the space. Home is about a sense of familiarity, but that isn't limited to being a familiar place. Home is also about people, about a feeling of belonging, about being with people who care for you and who you care for, too. Pico Iyer is an author, essayist, and travel writer who has lived all over the globe. He has a great TED Talk called "Where Is Home" in which he says, "And for more and more of us, home has really less to do with a piece of soil than, you could say, with a piece of soul. If somebody suddenly asks me, 'Where's your home?' I think about my sweetheart or my closest friends or the songs that travel with me wherever I happen to be."[2]

Creating a sense of home as you transition to school isn't just about making the space feel like your own, but about finding the people who will provide a sense of home as well. As I developed close relationships at school and became more comfortable living on my own and away from my family, there started to be more of a feeling of home at U of A for me, too, one that I initially felt guilty about. It felt like on some level I was betraying my family and our home. This was also how I felt about beginning to feel like my friends were also family. It took me some time to realize that I could have two locations that feel like home. Over time, I would wind up having many more locations resonate with me in different ways as I have continued to live in different places. This brings up another hard part of growing up, a growing realization that however much a place feels like home, it cannot cure us of sometimes feeling a sense of incredible loneliness. I find Frederick Buechner's description of this beautiful:

> That you can be lonely in a crowd, maybe especially there, is readily observable. You can also be lonely with your oldest friends, or your family, even with the person you love most in the world. To be lonely is to be aware of an emptiness that takes more than people to fill. It is to sense that something is missing which you cannot name.
>
> "By the waters of Babylon, there we sat down and wept, when we remembered Zion," sings the Psalmist (137:1). Maybe in the end it is Zion that we're lonely for, the place we know best by

---

2. Iyer, "Where Is Home," 2:42.

You're Not the Only One

longing for it, where at last we become who we are, where finally we find home.[3]

Buechner's words remind us that our souls find their temporary home here in this life, but that not until we dwell in the kingdom of God will we be in our true home. In this life, as wonderful as home can be, be that the home you grew up in or one you have created for yourself, a physical location or certain people, home is still flawed and can also be a place where we can experience loneliness or hurt. As we grow up, our understanding of home will change, too. Some of the ways we idealize our concept of home will drop away, yet there will remain deep within you a longing to just go home. There are still days I experience this—this longing to go home without even knowing exactly what that means or what I am longing for. Maybe it is a longing for Zion.

While there are times I long for home, there is also truth in that I have a choice in what my home will be. This is what Jesus is talking about in the passage from the Sermon on the Mount at the beginning of this chapter, which is often referred to as the "wise and the foolish builder." Though on the surface it is talking about two people who have built houses, one on a rock foundation and the other on sand, it isn't really talking about literal, physical houses. It comes at the end of three chapters of Jesus preaching what is known as the Sermon on the Mount. Jesus goes through one topic after another, after another, and each is something you can spend your entire life working on. At the end of all this he gets to this illustration, which begins by saying that everyone who acts on these words that Jesus has spoken will be like the wise builder who built his house on the rock. When the rains came, and the waters rose, the waters were not going to wash away the house that had been built on such a solid foundation. The foolish builder, who built his house on sand, did not have such a foundation, and when the rains came, according to the song I learned growing up, "the house on the sand went splat!" When we are able to create for ourselves a larger understanding of home, then we can see it as what we are building our life on, what makes up our foundation. In his TED Talk, Iyer says, "And home, in the end, is of course not just the place where you sleep. It's the place where you stand."[4] Where is it that you stand, and what is it that you stand on? How much does that really change because you are at college, and how

---

3. Buechner, *Whistling in the Dark*, 83.
4. Iyer, "Where Is Home," 13:28.

much does it stay the same? Are you building your life and home on the rock?

Prayer

God in whom we find our home,
We need your presence in our lives.
Leaving home can be hard.
Growing up can be hard, too.
Home is a place we are meant to feel safe, cared for, and loved.
Help us to find home where we are now,
To find the people and spaces that will provide us a home
From which we continue to go forth.
Help us to build our lives on you,
The solid rock,
And to know that with such a solid foundation we can weather the storm.
Be with us in our moments of loneliness,
The times when our souls long for a place beyond our knowing,
A place where you have made all things well, and all people whole.
Amen.

Reflection Questions

1. What was the home(s) you grew up in like? What are the parts of home you want to make sure are incorporated into the sense of home that you will create for yourself? What elements do you want to change?

2. Who are the people in your life who it feels like home to be with? What is it about them that creates this feeling?

3. What makes up the foundation on which you have constructed your life? How has that changed since you started college, and how has it stayed the same? What can you do to continue to make sure you can build your life on a solid foundation?

5

When What You Believe Changes

True mystery, the kind of mystery rooted in the infinite nature of God, gives us answers that actually plunge us into even more . . . questions.

—Rob Bell

But when [doubt] comes it seems so very real and frightening, as if your entire universe is going to fall apart.

—Donald Miller

I still have my questions and doubts, they don't just magically disappear, although right now I am at peace with them.

—My Thesis Journal

Scripture Reading

For we know only in part, and we prophesy only in part; but when the complete comes, the partial will come to an end. When I was a child, I spoke like a child, I thought like a child, I reasoned like a child; when I became an adult, I put an end to childish ways. For now we see in a mirror, dimly, but then we will see face to face. Now I know only in part; then I will know fully, even as I have been fully known. And now faith, hope, and love abide, these three; and the greatest of these is love. (1 Cor 13:9–13)

When What You Believe Changes

I've always been someone who asks a lot of questions. This includes asking questions about my faith. When we learned the Apostle's Creed for our Sunday school Bible goal in probably third or fourth grade, I remember asking the teacher, "If Jesus sits on the right hand of God, then who sits on the left?" I probably remember asking because I don't think I ever got an answer! By middle school, when I was a part of a Christian club that met at my public school and interacting with peers from churches whose theology was very different from my own, I remember having questions about why some churches didn't allow women to be in leadership and doubted that being male actually gave you any more authority in understanding God. I remember driving home from church with my mom in high school, asking questions about what happened to non-Christians when they died and not being able to accept that a loving God would be willing to damn 70 percent of the world's population, many of whom lived lives that better reflected what Jesus taught than some Christians.

So, it wasn't like I went to college having never asked questions before, including questions that were not easily answered. Going to college, however, is likely going to expose you to a wide array of people, subjects, and experiences in quantities unlike what you have encountered before and in ways that will force you to face and wrestle with some of the things you believe. This is not something to be afraid of.

Your religious beliefs are going to change in college. Actually, not just specific beliefs about your faith, but your thoughts and opinions on lots of things. And that's okay. It's not just okay, it's completely normal. It's part of growing up, of allowing your faith to become a more robust, adult faith. This will be a faith that will take you into the next stage of life. This is the faith you can claim as your own, not just what you have been taught and experienced at home and in the church where you grew up. God will always remain somewhat mysterious for us. We can know and understand God in part and in this have an incredible sense of who God is, but when we have faith in something that is utterly beyond our comprehension, we will never understand it completely and will always ask questions. Beginning to question things you have always believed to be true—sometimes things you think are critical to your faith—can be frightening though. You fear that it could be a slippery slope—if I let this belief change, then what will keep them all from changing, what will keep me from losing faith entirely? Just because your beliefs start to change doesn't mean you'll lose your faith, but it might come out at the other end looking a little different.

You're Not the Only One

In *Velvet Elvis*, a book I first read between my sophomore and junior years of college, Rob Bell talks about our faith using the metaphor of a brick wall and a trampoline. He describes some people as those whose faith is a type of "brickianity," a brick wall in which each brick represents a belief. If you start to take out some of those beliefs, the wall can come crashing down, and very little remains except a pile of rubble. He describes others whose faith is like a trampoline. Their faith is made of springs that are able to stretch, and bend, and change shape. If a couple of springs break entirely it's okay, because the trampoline as a whole still works. He also explores the inherent reason that each of these things exist. The point of a wall is to separate, to mark things as either being inside or outside, to divide what is okay from what's not. But the point of a trampoline is about something that is life-giving, that involves play and brings joy. It's also pretty easy to invite others to jump with us![1]

While I had been raised in a way that resembled the trampoline, I needed that trampoline faith as I journeyed through college. The first time in college that I remember when someone tried to directly challenge what they assumed I believed occurred the fall of my freshman year, at a Bible study no less. At the Bible study were myself, Pastor Ben (the campus minister for the PCM I was a part of), and Tim and Drew, two upper-class males who were good friends of each other. Tim seemed to want to make sure I knew I was a little freshman who knew nothing, while also challenging the authority of Ben, attitudes he carried beyond this one encounter. We were talking about the flood story—Noah, the ark, and the animals. Instead of engaging in a conversation about what we might learn from the story as it is told, Tim felt the need to explain that the flood story is actually two different stories by two different authors that have been combined to create the story we have today, and that when you separate them out using the Hebrew name for God used in each verse, you actually get two different stories that tell different tales than the combined one. He did this in a way that felt like he was trying to make me feel inferior in knowledge for not knowing this, and also challenge my faith, assuming that I must naively believe the literal words on the page. I don't remember if Drew engaged much in the conversation or not, but let's just say from what I recall that he didn't participate in any kind of meaningful way.

This experience challenged me in multiple ways. Here were two upper-class members of the campus ministry not demonstrating a spirit

---

1. Bell, *Velvet Elvis*, 18–36.

of Christian hospitality but being antagonistic and mean. It sucked, but I didn't want to let it get to me. I wanted to show him that I was not the person he was making me out to be. A few days later, I did process what had happened with Pastor Ben, which was helpful. Being around people who call themselves Christians while not seeking to lead a Christlike life is always painful, but it's important in those moments to remember all of those who are showing us Christ's love. In terms of the challenge to my faith that Tim sought to create, I'm pretty sure that at this point in my life the historical validity of the flood did not matter all that much to me and my faith. I had heard that every culture has some type of creation story and some type of flood story, and that what we see in the early chapters of Genesis are the Jewish and Christian version of these, so that didn't bother me. What I hadn't thought much about was the authorship of Genesis, and the idea of multiple authors having contributed to its pages was new to me. Even though the experience with Tim and Drew had been a negative one, I allowed it to become an opportunity for me to dig deeper into my faith. Rather than devastating my faith, this theory of multiple authors made me wonder. So I learned about it, in part from talking to Pastor Ben. Although how exactly these books were written remains a topic of intense discussion today, there are theories about who the various, possible authors might have been. This idea of multiple authors for a story that spans hundreds of years made sense to me, even if it was new. I also felt that who wrote them doesn't change God's involvement in the process. Wrestling with this my freshman year of college also helped prepare me for what was to come in seminary.

That was not the only time, however, the flood story got me thinking in a new way about my faith. During my junior year, in a course with Dr. Swaim, we read Gilgamesh, a flood narrative from ancient Mesopotamia that significantly pre-dates the narrative in Genesis. There are numerous similarities between the two stories, including a boat with pairs of every species of animal. I became intrigued as to what might be the reason that we do have these flood stories and decided to write a couple of papers on them that year, one for this class as well as one for another class. I did a significant amount of research, read about different flood theories, and found myself fascinated by the possibilities of what might have happened historically to cause the stories we have today. While the evidence that is left behind when a massive flood occurs does not exist for any kind of global event, research does point to the possibility of the Black Sea experiencing a catastrophic flood. To those living nearby, it would have seemed as if their whole world was impacted. That made sense to me, as did the fact that a culture would develop stories about that event, stories that warned future generations of a similar type of thing happening. I developed an understanding of some of these early stories in Genesis as our myths—stories that might not be factual events, but still contain a lot of truth—truth about humanity, human nature, and God. The springs on my trampoline were stretching, maybe changing shape, but they still worked.

What the flood story represents in my life is an encounter with new ideas—ideas that challenged some of what I had long accepted as true about the Bible and faith. It also represents how I chose to let a spring stretch, and in doing so it may have even found a way to work better. During her first lecture for the class in which we read Gilgamesh, I remember Dr. Swaim saying something really important to the class. On that first day, Dr. Swaim said to us that she didn't want this course to make any of us lose our faith, but she wanted us to be able to have our faith withstand being challenged and for us to be able to answer questions we might be asked about why we believed what we believed. The course was Early Roots of Christianity, and we spent the semester looking at writings from the centuries leading up to the time in which Jesus lived, writings that may have influenced how the story of Jesus was told, including Plato, Egyptian mythology, and the Hebrew Scriptures. The class was definitely challenging for me and figuring out what it meant for my faith as I learned about new ideas. The things we studied over the semester often seemed to directly challenge some of what we believe about Jesus, exposing me to where the same concepts and themes show up in earlier or concurrent mythologies, things like the virgin birth and resurrection. It was both frightening and comforting to hear Dr. Swaim tell us she wanted to test and strengthen our faith but not take it away. Now I know how incredibly important what she was trying to teach us really is. Our faith will be challenged, as it should be. We also need to take the time to not just blindly accept what we hear at church or read somewhere, but to really dig into what we believe ourselves and understand what matters to us and why. All of this is part of an active life of faith; we are never meant to have it all figured out. As I began my final semester of college, I wrote in my thesis journal, "One of the comments that has stayed with me is when Prof. Swaim said to me that though my beliefs might be changing, she knows that my faith is rock solid." Having faith also means having questions and growing and changing.

When What You Believe Changes

When you look at theories of faith development, a more mature faith is one that understands why it believes what it does and does not simply parrot back what one has been told they are supposed to believe. In order to truly understand and own your own faith, you often have to do some dismantling and reassembling, which is not always an easy or painless process. In the midst of this is a sense of loss, a loss of that childlike faith that Jesus speaks of, a loss of a more pure and simple way of understanding the world. As we become aware of adult realities, of new ideas, new responsibilities, and a growing awareness of world events, there are times when you may feel off-center or unbalanced. It can be hard for our faith—the thing that feels like it should be our anchor—to go through the process of becoming more complex, less simple and straightforward, and more gray than black and white. This has been something I have experienced personally and journeyed with many others through. One student first came to the CA after friends in other Christian groups had told her she needed to stop asking questions and just believe. Another had never had the opportunity to talk about what it means to be a Christian and believe in evolution. Each student has had their own unique journey. Ultimately, those who make this journey have a stronger, more resilient faith from doing the work.

This Scripture from 1 Corinthians seems to capture that well. It's kind of weird, talking about knowing only in part, but that actually represents our reality—in this life we will indeed know only in part, and not in full. As a child we are in a different developmental stage, one that some of us wish we never had to leave behind. Note that Paul says "childish," which is different from the child-like faith that Jesus praises and which does have strengths. The reality remains, we do have to grow up, and we need a faith that grows up with us if we want our faith to play a significant role in our adult lives.

My wish for you is that you experience what Dr. Swaim wished for those of us in her class—that you will be pushed and challenged, that your beliefs may be tested, and you might encounter things that make you ask big and deep questions, but that you do not lose your faith. I hope that you find the people to be on this journey with, both mentors and peers, knowing the pivotal role they have played in my journey.

I also hope you can learn to be comfortable with not having all the answers, with realizing that God is simply more vast than we can comprehend, that not everything has an answer, and that part of being people of faith is also being people who embrace mystery. In my thesis journal, I wrote, "Life is supposed to be a beautiful mystery, which leaves us in awe. Some people are so terrified by not having the answers that they create them. For me, I think the answers, or what answers can be found, lie tied up in something much bigger." Sometimes, I want to understand perfectly whatever that bigger thing is; in fact, this tortured me during part of the fall of my senior year. Other times, there is beauty in knowing that I can never fully understand it all, that I have to let go—of my desire for control, my desire to know, my desire to understand. In those moments, I can rest in the awesomeness of our creator, and believing that God is good, trust in the mysteries of faith.

Let's go back to Bell's metaphors. We build walls in part for safety, to minimize risk. Trampolines, on the other hand, involve risk. I loved jumping on the trampoline as a kid, though would feel a jolt of panic if I went too high. A lot of parents don't want to have a trampoline because kids may get injured, and yes, that does happen. A lot of us take the risk anyway and jump because of the experience. One of my favorite scenes in C. S. Lewis's *The Lion, the Witch, and the Wardrobe* is a conversation that occurs when the children meet Mr. and Mrs. Beaver. Having assumed Aslan to be a man, Mr. Beaver corrects their false assumption: "'Aslan is a lion—*the* Lion, the great lion.' 'Then he isn't safe?' said Lucy. 'Safe?' said Mr. Beaver; 'don't you hear what Mrs. Beaver tells you? Who said anything about safe? 'Course he isn't safe. But he's good.'"[2] What a wonderful description! It so well captures what it means to be truly living as a disciple of Jesus Christ—it may not make life entirely safe, but God is good. So take the risk, and go to places, both internally and externally, that may not seem safe. Let the questions in and the springs stretch. Embrace the mysteries of faith.

Prayer

God of mystery,
Be with us as we travel into new places in our faith,
Into areas and ideas unknown.
Be with us when we encounter things that challenge us,
And when we make new discoveries that excite us to the core.
Help us to make the transition to adulthood with grace,
And forgive those who seek to cause us to stumble along the way.
Let us find the life of discipleship to be a life of joy,

---

2. Lewis, *Lion*, 86.

And help us to have faith that more resembles a trampoline than a brick wall.
Guide us to the places that you would have us go,
Knowing that following you is not always the safest choice.
It may make us unpopular or different,
It may ask us to be prophetic,
It may demand that we make sacrifices of ourselves for others,
Or lead us to places we have never been.
But following you is worth the risk,
For you are good,
And you are love,
Which is the greatest thing of all.
Amen.

Reflection Questions

1. Do you resonate more with the idea of your faith as a brick wall, a trampoline, or something else? How have you experienced your own beliefs changing as you have grown up? What has that felt like? How have you responded?

2. What do you think Paul means when he says, "childish ways"? Childhood can represent innocence, but what else can it represent? What might it look like to outgrow your childish ways?

3. What scares you the most about what you believe changing? What excites you about having a faith that is dynamic? What are the core beliefs that you hold that you feel like must be true for you to keep your faith?

6

Do I Really Want to Call Myself "Christian"?

> Preach the gospel at all times, and, when necessary, use words.
> —Attributed to Francis of Assisi

> An unexamined, status-quo Christianity is not worth perpetuating. I cannot and will not stay Christian if it means perpetuating Christianity's past history and current trajectory.
> —Brian McLaren

Scripture

And Jesus came and said to them, "All authority in heaven and on earth has been given to me. Go therefore and make disciples of all nations, baptizing them in the name of the Father and of the Son and of the Holy Spirit, and teaching them to obey everything that I have commanded you. And remember, I am with you always, to the end of the age." (Matt 28:18–20)

Teacher, which commandment in the law is the greatest? He said to him, "'You shall love the Lord your God with all your heart, and with all your soul, and with all your mind.' This is the greatest and first commandment. And a second is like it: 'You shall love your neighbor as yourself.' On these two commandments hang all the law and the prophets." (Matt 22:36–40)

Do I Really Want to Call Myself "Christian"?

IF I'M COMPLETELY HONEST, there were times throughout college, and even some days still, where I struggle with the label "Christian." Then, and still today, I believe in Jesus Christ, but I don't want people to assume I'm one of those Christians—the Christian stereotype of close-minded, judgmental, and only caring about whether or not I'm saved and will spend eternity in heaven with Jesus. I don't want to be connected to people who believe that the role of women is to be submissive to men or be thought to be anti-LGBTQIA+. One of the hardest parts about Christianity for me is how diverse and disparate the range of Christian viewpoints and beliefs can be, even as I wonder if it is supposed to be this way. How can it be that there are Christians who are so completely different from me and what I believe? Sometimes, I feel like I have more in common with someone of a different faith than I do with someone from my own. Do I really want to use this label for myself that seems laden with so much baggage?

By the time I got to college, I had experienced plenty of interactions with the type of Christians that made me not want to use this label for myself, both people who I knew fairly well, and on several occasions, the random stranger. It was the encounters with people I did not know that I found far more invasive, and far less effective. The first time I remember being accosted by a stranger asking about my beliefs was when I was in high school. I had gone to see *Tuck Everlasting* with a couple of friends from church. As we walked out of the theater, we were stopped by a couple of girls about our age. They asked us if we believed in Jesus and if we went to church, to which we said yes. They then asked us if we listened to any non-Christian music. At that point, I was deep into a country music phase (I go in and out of these), so I said I listened to country as well as to Christian music. They asked if, when we listened to country, it made us want to get down on our knees and praise Jesus, and told us if we were truly Christian we would only listen to Christian music and not to any secular music. As we walked away, I thought that there is also a lot of Christian music that does not make me want to get down on my knees and praise Jesus, and that there was a decent amount of country music that did talk about faith and good values. To me, it seemed hard to justify their refusal to be exposed to the vast array of music that exists, some of which, while not Christian, was written for God. There is music in which the song writer is pondering religion and exploring their questions. I also had to wonder about classical music that didn't have words. Did they think that was acceptable? Or the many film scores that I listened to? On top of all of this, how was being that overtly judgmental of another person supposed to make them actually want to be a part of what you were trying to promote (which is something I still wonder)?

In college, I learned where the people with the surveys were. One of the campus ministry groups almost always had a few people standing in front of the library, asking those passing by if they had a couple minutes to take a survey. I tried to avoid them after deciding to take the survey once. I think there were about ten questions, asking if I knew God, asking if I was saved, asking if I wanted to talk more to someone to learn how to avoid going to hell. I talked to the student who gave me my survey for a couple minutes, but I really didn't need to be told about the benefits that having Jesus in my life would bring, which seemed to be all they were able to talk to me about, even when I tried to acknowledge we were both Christians and steer the conversation elsewhere. Everyone on campus knew who you meant if you talked about the people with the surveys, and not because they thought it was a good thing.

For me, one of the most frustrating aspects of my encounters with in-your-face Evangelical Christians has been their inability to have a conversation with you when they find out you, too, are a Christian, unless you are okay with a one-way conversation. One evening during my sophomore year of college, there was a knock on the door of my apartment, and when I answered, there was a man standing there. I don't remember exactly how he started his spiel, but he was a Christian and wanted me to be a Christian, too, and I think was also inviting me to his church. He probably started by asking if I had a relationship with Jesus, which I told him I did and that I actually planned to go to seminary and become a pastor. He had a bunch of Scripture verses he wanted me to hear, several of which were actually ones that I had memorized and completed aloud with him as he said them. But no matter what I said, he kept right on going with his script. I remember being disappointed that here was a person trying to tell people about Jesus, and when he encountered someone he could have a deeper conversation about faith with, he wasn't able to do so. That seemed to me to be a faith that lacked depth and richness.

Memorizing a script is not what faith in Jesus Christ is really about. When that is what is going around door-to-door, that is what some people, both non-Christians as well as people who came out of that culture, will think Christianity is, and I don't want to be associated with that. Nor do I want to be associated with people who stop those walking out of the movie

Do I Really Want to Call Myself "Christian"?

theater, and who judge their faith based on what radio station they have on or what their year-end listening stats look like. Nor do I want to be associated with the people standing outside of the library, supposedly concerned about the eternal destination of my soul but not necessarily caring about me right here and right now, a human being who might be having a wonderful or terrible day, a person who might be dying of loneliness and just looking for someone to connect with. If this is what Christianity is, I want no part in being connected with that, and I do not want to use the term "Christian" to describe myself.

But here's the thing—I do believe in Jesus, and I do go to church, and I do try to love God with all my heart, soul, and mind and to love my neighbor. I want people to know this about me, and I want them to see in it something appealing. In college, I wanted people to know that I was going to be a pastor, to give my life to serving Jesus, and that not all pastors fit their stereotypes. I wanted them to know that I believe that evolution is really a thing, that I contemplated if there is life on other planets and what the heck that would mean in terms of our salvation narrative, and that I thought being a Christian should be more about making sure all people are fed and clothed than solely caring about what they believe. I wanted people to know that I was a different kind of Christian than all of their stereotypes, that I had a living, breathing, growing faith, full of questions and doubts.

In one of Dr. Swaim's classes, she told us a story from when she was a college student herself, some fifty years before she stood before us that day. One day, the students were all sitting at their desks when the professor walked in. He grabbed a piece of chalk, and wrote the following on the board:

> Church-ianity—a bunch of politics
> Christianity—a bunch of theology
> Christ-likeness—the only thing that matters

Then he proceeded to turn around and begin his lecture on an entirely different topic. This has always remained with me because it gets at the heart of the matter. Are we living our lives in a way that witnesses to how Christ lived and taught us to live? That's what I love about the quote attributed to Francis of Assisi, which was my senior quote in my high school yearbook. I want my life to preach the gospel. I want my actions to witness to the love of God. I live my faith through how I live my life, through the choices I make, the ways that I choose to spend my time. And if someone were to ask me about my faith, sure, I'd talk about it.

You're Not the Only One

And yet. And yet I know deep down that this is not enough. I know that we do have to use words. I know that in a world where chaos too often seems to reign, where every week, sometimes every day, there seem to be headlines of awful events, we have to use words. Just not the same words as some of our fellow Christians use, words that focus on what will happen after we die. When too often it feels like hell is actually right here and right now, we need words of hope for today, not for when we're dead. When there are hundreds of mass shootings in the US each year, the climate is changing leading to more natural disasters and the potential extinction of species, and the "us versus them" mentality makes us fail to see one another as human beings; I need a faith that matters now. When many of the structures of racism and systemic oppression have been supported by, and sometimes even rooted in the church, we need a God who works outside of the box, who pushes us to change and see what God's kingdom looks like, and we need a faith that is going to work for change. We need a God who is in our midst, who is in the mess. As a Christian, that is indeed what I believe in. I want to share this with people! Not in a "believe what I believe or else be damned" kind of way, but in an "understand what is at the core of who I am and this is who the God I serve really is" kind of way. At a time where we have an ever-growing population of "nones"—people with no religious affiliation—it seems vital to witness to a thoughtful, integrated kind of faith, a faith that actually has a relevance in the here and now and points toward a God who is concerned with the lost and the least, those on the margins. I've yet to hear this coming through a bullhorn.

The final verses in Matthew, known as the Great Commission, is the passage in Scripture at the heart of all this. Jesus tells the disciples to go to the ends of the earth, teaching people to practice everything he has taught them. That's a pretty daunting task, but I also believe that if we really did that, really taught people to live how Jesus commanded us to live, which has very little to do with salvation after our death, this would be a good thing. Jesus told us if we have two coats to share one with someone who has none and to not be anxious about the future. He told us to love God and our neighbor, whoever that neighbor may be, as well as to love our enemy. If we lived as Jesus called us to live, the world would look so incredibly different than it does today, and we would get to experience the kingdom of God, the world as God intended it to be and promises that it can still be. Which is why I paired this verse with how Jesus responds when he is asked what is the greatest commandment, because if we could live those out and

Do I Really Want to Call Myself "Christian"?

share those with others, I think we would help people to be more Christ-like, which maybe is the only thing that really matters.

You have likely grown up in a pluralist society, being exposed to people from many different backgrounds, including different faiths traditions. Just as I believe that there needs to be diversity within Christianity, I also believe that with the amount of beautiful diversity in so many elements of life, there have to be diverse ways of knowing our creator. As I love God and love my neighbor, I respect my neighbor for who they are and for what they believe. I believe they can show me truths about God I may not have seen in my limited understanding, and I might likewise show them truths they may not have seen before. This doesn't mean I hide my own faith though; it means I own it and I share it, while also allowing them space to own and share their own faith. Sometimes those who are not Christian show us the best examples of how to live as Christ taught us to live! This can feel confusing and defy our expectations. It's not my job to make sense of it all, but to listen to God wherever God speaks. The relationships I have with people of other faiths have broken down some of my stereotypes and prejudices, have shown me other ways that people live out their faith, and led to so many enriching conversations. Part of these relationships is acknowledging that yes, we have some different beliefs and that's okay.

These are things I think many of us think about and wrestle with, including many students I've worked with. Several years ago, shortly after Easter, a student named Alyssa wrote this for the CA's blog:

> I'll freely admit a lot of the time, especially here at Penn, I don't boldly proclaim myself as a child of God. When people ask me where I'm going Wednesday afternoons sometimes I say to a meeting and don't clarify that with a meeting of the Christian Association student board. When people ask me where I'm working this summer sometimes I just say my camp, not Lutheridge, an ELCA Lutheran summer camp.
>
> I don't hide these things because I'm embarrassed or shy about my faith, I'm a proud follower of Jesus Christ. Sometimes, though, I assume that there will be judgments, meaning I assume that people will be turned off from me. That people don't care for people affiliated with the church or with religion in general. I feel like I'm not alone in this, especially on a busy, pragmatic, and for me often not spiritual campus like ours. But if we can put those fears aside, if we can boldly proclaim the children of God we are called to be, there's no telling the difference we can make in the lives of others and in the world.

When we cast those fears of judgment and misunderstanding aside we can be part of reframing peoples opinions of who and what Christians are and who Christ was and is. We can proclaim our loving grace-filled God to our campus and to the world! But this can't be achieved by actions alone. Our words and bold proclamations of faith have to accompany our actions of love and compassion. When they do, we can be living, breathing manifestations of the Risen Lord. In this season of Easter I challenge all of us to get better at using our words to reveal ourselves as children of God.[1]

May this be a challenge we each set for ourselves as well.

Prayer

Jesus Christ, Bringer of Peace,
We give thanks that we call you not only our savior,
But our teacher, brother, and friend.
We love you and believe in you and what you came to teach us.
Sometimes it feels like we as people have perverted your message,
Making us question if we want to be associated with the religion that claims to follow you.
Help us to know how to show the world that we do believe in you,
That we believe you offer a radical love and grace we cannot comprehend,
That you broke barriers and challenged the status quo,
And that following you is not about judgment or sin,
But about bringing an incredible hope to the world,
A hope for a world in which all people treat one another with love and respect,
And work together to make sure that all of your children and creations are cared for.
Give us the courage to show with our actions and our words that we are your followers.
Amen.

---

1. Kaplan, "Proclaiming God's Love."

Do I Really Want to Call Myself "Christian"?

Reflection Questions

1. Are there times you do not want to call yourself a Christian? Why do you think that is the case? What stereotypes of Christians do you not want to be associated with? Have you experienced public Christian behaviors that don't feel Christian to you?

2. What are some of the ways you have handled, or could imagine handling, getting a negative reaction to you being a Christian? How would it differ if it came from a friend versus a stranger?

3. How can we verbally share our faith with others in a way that we also feel comfortable with? Why might sharing our faith verbally help us to grow in our own faith? How do you imagine it might feel? What are the words you might use?

4. If we are witnessing to our faith through our actions, what does that mean? How might this influence the choices we make, in how we choose to live our lives, while always remembering that grace abounds?

7

Finding a Faith Community

No Church Is Going to Be Exactly Like Your Home Church

To eat this particular meal together is to meet at the level of our most basic humanness, which involves our need not just for food but for each other. I need you to help fill my emptiness just as you need me to help fill yours. As for the emptiness that's still left over, well, we're in it together, or it in us. Maybe it's most of what makes us human and makes us brothers and sisters.

—Frederick Buechner

We have all known the long loneliness and we have learned that the only solution is love and that love comes with community.

—Dorothy Day

Scripture Reading

Let love be genuine; hate what is evil, hold fast to what is good; love one another with mutual affection; outdo one another in showing honor. Do not lag in zeal, be ardent in spirit, serve the Lord. Rejoice in hope, be patient in suffering, persevere in prayer. Contribute to the needs of the saints; extend hospitality to strangers. Bless those who persecute you; bless and do not curse them. Rejoice with those who rejoice, weep with those who weep. Live in harmony with one another; do not be haughty, but associate with the lowly; do not claim to be wiser than you are. Do not repay anyone evil for evil, but take thought for what is noble in the sight of all. If it is possible, so far as it depends on you, live peaceably with all. . . .

Do not be overcome by evil, but overcome evil with good. (Rom 12:9–18, 21)

I LOVED THE CHURCH I grew up in; it was like a second home for me. When I would come home from college, the first place I went was as often to church as it was to my house. This was in large part because my mom was often at work there as the senior high youth director, so there was a chance that if it was a Friday afternoon, no one would be at home if I went there. But it wasn't just that. I really did feel at home at church. Even if my mom was busy, I knew all the staff and would be happy to sit and talk with them or be put to work by them. My family started attending Mt. View Presbyterian Church before I can remember, back when I was one year old, so I grew up there. I can still sing the songs I learned in children's choir and remember some of the Sunday school Bible goals I learned over the years. The founding pastor of the church, Rev. Ralph Meredith, was there for twenty-nine years before he retired while I was in seminary. Over the years, a number of associate pastors came and went, many of whom I also got to know well, but Ralph was always there while I was part of the congregation. Ralph taught me a great deal about being a pastor through his words and actions, including how he got to know the children and youth of the church.

The church also felt like home because it acted as a type of extended family for us. My parents had moved to Phoenix from the Midwest when I was young, and our extended family remained in Kansas and Illinois. I knew most of the church community, at least the people who had been attending for a long time. Even if someone didn't know me personally, they at least typically knew that I was Buzzy's daughter (people always were looking for my mom for one reason or another!). I knew the rhythms of Mt. View, the flow of the service, the sounds of the choir, what would happen for holidays and significant days on the church calendar. I knew the services that were some of the most spiritually significant for me each year, and the things that happened that my sister and I might mimic at home (a few of which we still can do and laugh at today but will not be put in print). I knew that Bill would sit in the pew in front or behind us and write the name of some NFL player or actor or something funny in the attendance pad. When the Christmas tree got put up, you would hope none of the dove ornaments had fallen off and looked like a dead dove on the ground, making it almost impossible to look at the pastor and keep a straight face since the tree was next to the pulpit. You knew the eleven p.m. service on Christmas Eve was the service most of the students home from college would be at, and it was always exciting to see people there you hadn't seen in months. Mt. View was an integral part of my life.

In many ways, my family centered our lives around the church, and not just when my mom started working there. My dad sang in the church choir and volunteered with the youth group before my mom became the youth director (and continued to volunteer after as well). I attended Sunday school and sang in the children's choir. When they added a dinner on Wednesday nights, we ate there pretty much every week before choir or Bible study. We had a large and active youth group, and I served on the youth leadership team. By the time I left for college, the church had grown a lot. It was large for a Presbyterian church, with close to 1,200 members, so while I knew a lot of people, I by no means knew everyone anymore. I went to church almost every Sunday. It was part of the rhythm of life. I was known at church. They were people who had watched me grow up, people who helped to notice, name, and nurture my gifts and talents.

My family also developed a group of families we met at church who we spent all of the holidays with. They really were like aunts, uncles, and cousins. Depending on the season of life, the group changed a little, but there were four other families with whom we spent almost every Thanksgiving Day, Christmas Eve, Easter, and a variety of other occasions. The kids ranged over twelve years, and there were about thirteen of us. Though we thought we wanted to graduate to the adult table someday, by the time we were old enough, we realized we were just as happy having a kids' table! Then we could eat faster than the adults and get on to playing games. We rotated houses for each holiday. This chosen family gave us all a great group of adults who cared about us and lived faithful lives.

Then I went to college. I knew that I wasn't going to find Mt. View, but I also didn't know what it was like to try to find a new church. There were things that excited me about being able to go to a place where no one knew me. It was going to be nice to get to just be in a church and be able to slip out right when the service ended and not have things to do, people to talk to, and people asking me where they could find my mom. While in many ways the anonymity of a new church was appealing, it was also going to be weird not knowing anyone, not having people to catch up with about the past week, not having youth group to go to. I also didn't know how much time and work it takes to really feel like you belong in a new community, nor was I prepared to get used to new rhythms and new ways of doing things in addition to the new rhythms of college that involved many more late Saturday nights. But I knew I needed a spiritual home, a place to find community, be nourished, and continue to grow in my faith.

I immediately got involved with the PCM when I got to campus, which would serve as my primary faith community for the next four years. It was the community I committed to, built relationships in, and where I felt like I had a pastor. PCM worshiped on Tuesday nights, so on Sunday mornings I was free to find a church to attend, and with church having played such an important part in my life, I wanted to go. One of my friends from Mt. View lived in the same dorm I was in my freshman year. She was a sophomore who also had a car, so I started to check out Presbyterian churches down in Tucson. Some Sundays we would go to church together, others she let me borrow her car, and a fair number I just slept in after finishing up with marching band and football games well past midnight. It was hard to find something that felt "right." I remember one church where the people were incredibly friendly and even gave me a little loaf of homemade bread, but it was so different from what I was used to—it had under one hundred in worship and everyone knew everybody (something I've gotten much more used to now)! Another seemed good, except that the service lasted close to two hours, which was so different from the kept-to-an-hour service that I was used to at the time. There was another I liked but it was a little too far away, and another was progressive, but seemed a little too focused on progressive politics for me at the time.

I realize I sound a bit like Goldilocks here trying to find the church that's just right, and it can be hard to know when what we are looking for makes sense or when it may be slightly unrealistic. Finally, I found a church that I liked, which in some ways also reminded me of Mt. View, at the end of my freshman year, but by the end of sophomore year, I felt like I needed something different to nourish my soul. I decided not to switch immediately since there was only one semester left before I studied abroad. PCM had also started doing church visits at least a few Sundays each semester, where we helped to lead the worship service at some of the churches that helped to support our ministry. I often went on those visits and sometimes helped lead the liturgy. My senior year, I did more of this as well as sometimes attending another different church near campus, but outside of PCM, I never really found a church home in Tucson.

Studying abroad at the University of East Anglia in Norwich, England, gave me a different experience of church as well. The couple times I went to Reformed churches in Norwich, which is their version of the Presbyterian church, I was way younger than most people there, and the hymns were different too! I did go to evensong at the cathedral a few times, which I had not experienced before and liked. One of the nice things about my abroad experience was that I was able to spend Easter with a family my dad knew from work. When the father of the family picked me up at the train station on the evening of Maundy Thursday, he apologized that we would be going straight to church. I responded with how that made it feel like home! Spending that weekend engaging with their Holy Week and Easter traditions made it special, allowing me to experience a slight variation on something that also felt incredibly familiar.

In many ways, the whole experience of finding a church during college was kind of weird. Church had always meant being deeply involved in the community, and while to some extent the anonymity was indeed refreshing, not being known was also just strange. That community started to form for me through the campus ministry, but I also was used to and valued the intergenerational community that you find in a church. At the same time, it was hard to find the time, and to be honest, the energy, to really engage with a church community in order to develop the sense of belonging I had always felt at church. As a campus minster, I have had students at the CA struggle with whether or not they wanted to find a church congregation to worship with and potentially join. For some, they found what they were looking for at the CA and did not seek anything more. Others have gotten fully involved with local congregations, including being a part of the lay leadership in these churches.

For those who do want to find a church community, you may want to do a little research. What denomination was the church you grew up in, and do you want something similar or not? That can be a good place to decide which congregations you want to check out. Then, you want to find a congregation where you feel welcomed, where the worship service provides nourishment, and the sermons or messages provide both comfort and challenge. You may want to look at how the congregation is involved with the community and how they engage with issues that matter. Being the only young person doesn't mean you shouldn't stay, but you also may want

Finding a Faith Community

a congregation that other college students attend. If something doesn't feel right, if it feels off, pay attention to that, and if the church asks anything of you that makes you uncomfortable, find a different church. Especially around college campuses, high-pressure or cult-like groups will sometimes try to prey on students, which I say not to scare you but to help you be aware. Church should both nourish us spiritually and help us grow as disciples, and it is important to put some effort into finding the right community for this.

I don't think there is a right or a wrong way to go about figuring this out during your college years, but I strongly believe that it is important to be a part of some type of community of faith. One student from the CA was a part of our community, and then on Sundays would watch the video of worship from her home congregation across the country where she would attend when she was home on breaks, allowing her to feel connected to her community even when she was far away. Many more churches now offer their services online since having to go virtual during the COVID-19 pandemic, and keeping that connection can be nice. Others want a church where they can be physically present. For others, just being involved with a campus ministry is plenty for this season. Whichever might feel right for you, I truly believe we were created, even designed, to be in community, and that it's important for you to find something, even if you are questioning everything about this whole faith thing.

In the Epistles, which are letters written to early church communities, we find a great deal about how we should go about living in community and how we should treat one another. That is what we find in the passage from Romans here. How do you want to find a space to practice faithful community while in college? I know there are weeks where you have too much to do, or Sunday mornings where it seems impossible to get out of bed before noon, and finding a new faith community, especially a church, can be hard. I also know we shouldn't just put our faith on the back burner for four years, and so I encourage you to find something and attend when you can. If you're an introvert like me, put yourself out there. Don't be afraid to check out multiple congregations or campus ministries, including ones that belong to different denominations than the one you might have grown up in. If your needs change in college, find a new community that better reflects or speaks to your evolving faith.

No community is going to live out this Romans passage perfectly, and no community is perfect. Sometimes we see that better when we are removed, but sometimes we look back with rose-colored glasses and forget the flaws that were there. Sometimes we will return home to find a church that has changed (Mt. View today is a drastically different church then when I was growing up, and no longer a part of the Presbyterian Church [USA] denomination) or to find that we ourselves have changed and no longer feel that sense of belonging there. When Jesus returned to the synagogue in his hometown, they couldn't accept who he had become and thought he was crazy. Many of the students I've known at the CA have experienced shifts towards more progressive beliefs while in college or grad school. Still, while our communities may change, we were created to be in community, created in the image of God—Father, Son, and Holy Spirit, three-in-one and one-in-three. God, in God's very nature, is communal, is relationship. Community in all its iterations is good, but find one that tends to your soul, that reminds you that you are created in the image of God, one that provides a place for you to belong and helps you grow in discipleship along the way.

Prayer

Triune God,
In your very essence,
You are communal,
You are relationship.
You created us not to be alone,
But to be together,
To be communities that nurture,
Support, sustain, and care for one another.
You know it is hard for us to leave the communities we grew up in,
To move away from the places where we are known,
Accepted, and loved.
You know it is scary to walk into a room where we know no one,
And they do things differently than we are used to things being done.
Open us to new experiences,
To opportunities for new relationships,
To new practices that we could find even more meaningful,
That could provide us with new perspectives on the familiar.
Lead us to the communities you would have us be a part of,
To the places that will help us to grow,
And provide us somewhere to belong,
Somewhere we can worship you,

Finding a Faith Community

And be reminded of your love for us.
Amen.

REFLECTION QUESTIONS

1. What was the church you grew up in like? Did you have a strong connection to one congregation, or were you involved with several over the course of your childhood? What did you like about these congregations? What bothered you about them?

2. What do you look for in a church? Are there things that you want to see that help you know this is a community you want to be a part of? Are there things that turn you off? Should these be a deal breaker or not?

3. Why do you think it is important to be a part of a faith community? Is this something you prioritize? If not, why? What is something you can do to help make this more of a priority in your life?

8

Finding Your "Family"

The greatness of a community is most accurately measured by the compassionate actions of its members.
—Coretta Scott King

Safe. When I'm with you I feel so safe. Like I'm home.
—Andrew to Sam, *Garden State*

The soul needs to interact with other people to be healthy.
—Donald Miller

When I speak of love I am not speaking of some sentimental and weak response. I am speaking of that force which all of the great religions have seen as the supreme unifying principle of life. Love is somehow the key that unlocks the door which leads to ultimate reality.
—Martin Luther King Jr.

Scripture

As God's chosen ones, holy and beloved, clothe yourselves with compassion, kindness, humility, meekness, and patience. Bear with one another and, if anyone has a complaint against another, forgive each other; just as the Lord has forgiven you, so you also must forgive. Above all, clothe yourselves with love, which binds everything together in perfect harmony. And let the peace of

Christ rule in your hearts, to which indeed you were called in the one body. And be thankful. Let the word of Christ dwell in you richly; teach and admonish one another in all wisdom; and with gratitude in your hearts sing psalms, hymns, and spiritual songs to God. And whatever you do, in word or deed, do everything in the name of the Lord Jesus, giving thanks to God the Father through him. (Col 3:12–17)

VALENTINE'S DAY OF MY senior year of college is one of those dates I will probably always remember. Not because of some wonderful date—I didn't have a boyfriend—but because of the ways it captures the ups and downs of life with people that you love. Sometime during that day, I had heard about the school shooting at Northern Illinois University (NIU); another school shooting, tragic and yet no longer shocking. I went to the U of A basketball game that night with some friends when I got a text from Erin, a close friend from PCM, asking if I was free and could come over. Erin's dorm was close to the basketball stadium, so after the game I headed over to her dorm. While NIU seems far off from Tucson, Arizona, Erin grew up in Chicago. As I walked into Erin's room, I learned that not only did Erin know people at NIU, one of the young women she knew had been shot in the stomach and was in critical condition. There's not much you can do in that situation, other than just be there, be present. I stayed at Erin's for a little over an hour, talking about the incident and how she was feeling, and talking about stuff that was totally unrelated but could get her mind thinking about other things. We were reminded of the fragility of life, and that news headlines are not actually as anonymous as they feel but can be about people you know or could even be about you. It's a scary reality to face, and one we shouldn't have to face alone.

It was getting late, though, and at some point I got a text from my housemate Cassie asking when I would be home. When I got home, Cassie was in her room, and Mike and Shad were down on the couch in Mike's room. It was straight across from the door so you could see them down the hall and was where the two of them spent probably close to half of their time at the house that year, mostly playing *World of Warcraft*. I went into Cassie's room to talk about her day, what had happened with Erin, etc. There had been a lot of discussion leading up to Valentine's Day about whether or not her boyfriend was going to get her flowers, but he had, and they were gorgeous. Throughout our conversation, Cassie had been trying to drop hints that I should go into my room, and I think she eventually just bluntly told me to. I went in, put my bag down, but took a minute to notice the bouquet of beautiful tangerine-colored miniature roses sitting on my desk. Next to them sat a homemade card with a note from Shad and Mike. Cassie was standing in the doorway, watching my reaction. It was the sweetest thing they could have done and made me feel so loved by my very dear friends and roomies at the end of a long, hard day, a day that had made me question the goodness of humanity while sitting in the ripples of grief caused by a gunman's shooting spree. With something as simple as a bouquet of flowers meant to keep me from feeling lonely on this romantic holiday, they reminded me of humanity's goodness, of the ways in which people really can bring joy to others' lives. There was more to the story too. I would learn that Shad originally went to the store to get the flowers and got some red tulips. I think they had somehow used Cassie to find out that tulips are my favorite flower. But the tulips were droopy, and when Mike saw them he knew they wouldn't work and so had gone back to get the roses. It was thoughtful and special, and I still have that card saved with my keepsakes.

These are some of the people who in college became part of my chosen family. It didn't happen overnight, and it didn't happen without transition or grieving some of what was getting left behind with my childhood. The Valentine's Day I just described took place in my final semester, so let's back up and look at how I got there.

Some of us go to college believing that we are going to quickly find our new "best friends," the people we will do everything with for the next four years, the people who will be in our wedding. It might be our roommate, or people on our hall, or maybe someone we will meet in a club or sorority or fraternity. Sometimes this happens, and sometimes it doesn't. Both at college and in grad school, my friend groups would change and shift. There were people I connected with freshman year, people I would hang out and do stuff with, but they weren't quite yet my people. As I mentioned earlier, it took me awhile to find close friends in college. I had one close friend from church who was also a freshman, and we would get dinner together each week. Otherwise, almost all of the people I ended up closest with, my PCM family, weren't there my freshman year. Shad and Mike both started at other schools, and then transferred to U of A. My closest female friends from college are all a year or two years younger than me, so started after I did. We started getting to all know each other in the fall of sophomore

Finding Your "Family"

year. Once I started to develop a close group of friends in college, a group that would become my family, we started doing lots together, of which I have many memories. By spring of sophomore year, we started having our own lock-ins, or sleepovers, at the Campus Christian Center (CCC). We'd stay up talking or playing games—I remember one night involved Pictionary and lots of drawings of food, which I'm guessing may be when we did the "30 Hour Famine" and were being inspired by our hungry stomachs! Often, on Saturday morning when we'd get up, we would all go volunteer at the food bank and then come back to the CCC and make pancakes. I also naturally would become closer with some of the people in the group than with others, which I think was true for all of us. We each had close friendships with other people, too, making a kind of "extended family" of sorts. Sometimes when I feel a little anxious about my students now and wonder what mischief they might be getting up to together, I remind myself that I was once them, hanging out at weird hours at the CCC just enjoying one another's company.

It was at the beginning of junior year that Cassie, Mike, Shad, and I decided that we all were going to live together the following year. We decided this despite the fact that Cassie and I had just discovered Shad and Mike did not have what I would consider the best taste in movies! Two weekends in a row we had movie nights together. Two weekends in a row, Cassie and I decided we would let the guys choose the movie (why, I don't remember, except that I was exhausted from marching band and probably did not have much energy to do otherwise). This is the reason I have seen both *Team America* and *The Family Guy Movie*, neither of which I would have ever watched on my own or need to see a second time. But sitting on that couch, watching those awful movies, I found that I felt at home. I had found the people I would choose to be my family.

For a long time, maybe throughout the rest of college, there was a tension I felt about having these two places where I felt at home, these two places where I now had "family." I loved being able to spend time with my biological family, and it was always great to be with them. During my first year of college, it was hard to leave Phoenix to go back to school; I wanted to stay home. But as college progressed, at the end of a weekend in Phoenix I was sad to leave my family but often excited to return to this other place that now was also home. Ultimately, this was all good stuff, this is what is supposed to happen, and it's part of growing up; but at least for me, there was almost a sense of guilt that came with it, like I was betraying the family

I had grown up with. As I look back a few years later, I better understand that this is part of what the college experience is about. We need friends and we need community. We also need more than that, we need people in our lives who are our family. While technology has made it much easier for those of us who want to stay in close contact with our families of origin to do so, we also need people who are present where we now live. When I use the term "family," I mean people we can be around and feel like we don't have to put on any airs, people who truly love us and will still be there even after we take out our anger or frustration on them when we're in a bad mood. I mean people we are willing to risk having difficult conversations with because we'd rather get through something together than let it drive us apart. What I eventually realized was that I didn't need to be worried about this transition, even if it meant things were changing. This new family of choice isn't going to replace anybody. They will simply add to the wonderful family you now get to construct for yourself.

Once we lived together, it was even more clear that these people were family. It seemed like Erin was at the house as much time as she wasn't there, and there were a few others who were connected through a close friendship with at least one of us. Mike and Shad developed some special nicknames for me. We took care of each other, wanting each other to be healthy and happy, bearing with one another through difficult times. I remember walking into the CCC one day and Pastor Ben came out of his office and said something like, "Hi Megan. So I hear you don't sleep." I was a little perplexed and responded, "No, I sleep. Maybe not a lot, but I do sleep." It turned out Shad and Mike had told him they didn't think I slept, probably somewhat jokingly, but when he said that I could see they had a point. Truth was, I probably wasn't getting enough sleep that year because I both wanted to spend time with my friends and get my schoolwork totally done. I would stay up until around midnight with Mike and Shad, and then get up around 6:00 a.m. or 6:30 a.m. most mornings to do homework, well before they were awake. The fact that they noticed this and actually said something to Ben made me pay attention to what they had said and feel like they cared about me!

I also remember a different evening when I was in tears. Until recently, I had forgotten what they were even about, but I found something that reminded me it was a grade I had just gotten back that I was unhappy with. What I've always remembered is how my housemates responded. We were supposed to be making dinner together, but it's hard to cook when you have tears streaming down your face. So Cassie sat in the kitchen and talked to me while Shad quietly made dinner. After we ate, as Cassie and I kept talking, he quietly did all the dishes. I strongly felt that both of them took care of me that night, each in their own wonderful way. Although small acts of kindness may seem inconsequential, they are far from it. They are what help connect us to one another in a world that so often seems so vast and overwhelming and too often chaotic. It doesn't need to be just how we respond to a friend who is upset, but can be a text asking how you're doing, an unexpected chocolate or cup of coffee from a friend, or someone offering to stay up with you to keep you company while you finish your paper at the library. These are all reminders that we are not alone but are on this journey of life together with others.

One of my favorite parts of living together, and maybe one of the most important, was when we would all cook and have meals together. The table is a sacred space, and in the preparation and the sharing of a meal we would be fully present to one another, as well as often just having a good time. There have been occasional moments in my life that have seemed almost transcendent in the sense that I was both in the moment and also observing it happen at the same time, for just a matter of seconds. This happened one night during my senior year as we were preparing dinner. Simultaneously, I was in the moment and yet also felt like I was watching us, fully aware that I wanted to be as present as I could to moments like these, which were going to end all too soon when Shad and I graduated at the end of the year. This was such a sacred moment, a space where I could experience what God's love feels like.

The Scripture from Colossians is one that you often hear read at weddings, but it's meant for a community. For the majority of us, we were raised within a family that was not of our choosing, and the people in that family helped shape who we are today. But then there is the family we get to choose, those friends who will become so close they feel like more than friends. This community is important, and so is how we treat one another within it. This passage encourages us to share life together, the joys and triumphs, the successes, the setbacks, and the screwups. It's about how to live life as a Christian community, how to become better disciples together, and build one another up along the way.

Relationships like these need time and care, so let me share a couple of thoughts about tending to our relationships. Hopefully the shifts in life during the COVID-19 pandemic taught us many things, but one of the things it taught us was that our friendships matter, that being cut off from being able to be together in person is tough on our wellbeing. Sure, we did stuff virtually, but nothing is the same as being with our people. Community is vital to our mental health. Friendships take work, and pandemic or not, we need to put time into these relationships. We've all experienced feeling like a friend doesn't have time for us, and that is a painful experience, even if it's just for a season. So, my other piece of advice is, if you fall head over heels in love with someone, don't forget about your friends. Whether that person ends up your future spouse or breaks your heart, you're going to need your friends, and that other person is also going to need their friends. It's so easy to get caught up in that romantic relationship and feel like it's your entire world, but don't let it be. Whatever life brings, you're going to need your people, your community.

Of all the friends I had in college, it's the PCM family that I have stayed connected to. I catch up with a number of them on occasion. We're trying to gather in person more often now, but in between, we catch up by phone or email, and we all watch what's going on in each other's lives on social media and through Christmas cards. The group has changed over the years—some are now married, and there are more than a handful of kids and counting. Over the years, the weddings have been reunions for those able to make it, and we have now had a couple of reunions to see each other and talk of doing another. It still feels natural to be together. These are the kinds of friends and family it's worth spending some time to find because they are with you for the long haul.

PRAYER

Triune God,
Who in your very essence is community,
Thank you for all of the people in our lives.
Thank you for the family from which we come.
Allow us to celebrate all that was good,
And to heal from what was not.
Be with us as we go to school,
Leaving our family and friends from back home,
Sometimes feeling like we are starting over,
Wanting people to like us and want to be our friend.
Guide us to those who will become our chosen family,
Who will go with us through good and bad times,

Finding Your "Family"

Who we will laugh and cry with,
And who will care enough about us to let us know when they are concerned.
When we have found those people,
Help us to nurture those relationships,
To give them the time and attention they deserve.
Help us to clothe ourselves with compassion, kindness,
humility, meekness, patience, and love.
Amen.

REFLECTION QUESTIONS

1. What was your relationship with your family like before you went to college? Were you close with your parents or siblings? Were you ready to get out of the house and go to school?

2. How did meeting people at college compare to your expectations of what it would be? Have your friends changed since you got to college? What was that experience like?

3. Do you have friends you feel like you can count on in difficult times? Do these friends feel like family to you? What do you think makes it feel that way?

4. What do you look for in a person who you might consider to be part of your college family?

9

Will You Be My Mentor?

A mentor is someone who allows you to see the hope inside yourself.
—Oprah Winfrey

My mentor said, "Let's go do it," not "You go do it." How powerful when someone says, "Let's!"
—Jim Rohn

If I have seen further it is by standing on the shoulders of giants.
—Isaac Newton

Scripture

So he set out from there, and found Elisha son of Shaphat, who was plowing. There were twelve yoke of oxen ahead of him, and he was with the twelfth. Elijah passed by him and threw his mantle over him. He left the oxen, ran after Elijah, and said, "Let me kiss my father and my mother, and then I will follow you." . . .

And as they still went on and talked, behold, chariots of fire and horses of fire separated the two of them. And Elijah went up by a whirlwind into heaven. And Elisha saw it and he cried, "My father, my father! The chariots of Israel and its horsemen!" And he saw him no more. He picked up the mantle of Elijah that had fallen from him, and went back and stood on the bank of the Jordan. He took the mantle of Elijah that had fallen from him, and struck the water, saying, "Where is the Lord, the God of Elijah?" When he had struck the water, the water was parted to the one side and to the other, and Elisha went over. When the company of prophets who were at Jericho saw him at a distance, they declared, "The spirit of Elijah rests on Elisha." (1 Kgs 19:19–20; 2 Kgs 2:11–15)

WE ALL NEED PEOPLE in our lives who can show us the way, teach us how to do things, help us be who we are, and learn how to live. We need people we can turn to, people who are not just friends, but who are mentors. We benefit from people in our lives who have more wisdom than we do, more life experience. What this means during your time at college is that you need to seek out adults to develop these types of relationships with, adults who care about you and get to know who you are as a person. My parents are great, and I had and have a wonderful relationship with them, but these need to be people other than your parents, people who are outside the sphere of the pre-college you. They might be a professor, a campus minister, a coach or music director, maybe the person in charge of your dorm, or a club or Greek-life advisor.

It is likely going to be the case that they will not come looking for you or magically show up on your doorstep (that would be creepy if someone literally did, but, I mean, don't expect an email to show up in your inbox). You will need to make an effort, to show up at office hours, and show up again, or ask if they have time to meet with you outside of their normal office hours if you have a conflict. Even if it's not a professor or someone who has set office hours, ask if you could meet with the person. If you don't hear back, ask again; it doesn't necessarily mean their answer is no when they often are buried in emails and may have missed yours. Penn now has this fantastic program (and I hope some other schools do as well) where students can take a mentor to lunch (along with a couple other students as well, if wanted), and the school covers all the meals (it's in a nice, cafeteria-style dining area). You might even be explicit in your intentions, saying that you are looking for their guidance on more than just an assignment or the class. You'll find some people are very interested in only their field, but there is likely still a role for them to play, and others can help with bigger questions like deciding what to do with your life. Put in the time and energy to find some of these people at college. Believe me when I say it's worth it! It will make for better reference letters at the very least, but will likely, and more importantly, provide you with meaningful relationships.

I want to share with you who some of those people were for me during my college years, and a little about them and why they mattered so much to my experience. These four people all had different roles to play but shaped me in ways that continue today. At the time I met each of them, they ranged in age from late twenties to early seventies, and one has since passed away. Telling you about them makes this chapter long, but is my thank you to them and an acknowledgement of how big of a role your mentors can play. After, I'll talk more about what to look for in a mentor and some of my experiences as I've now served as a mentor for others as well.

Professor Rees

To put it short, Rees kicked my butt. Well, technically, he made me run it back and do it again so many times that my butt felt like it had been kicked. Professor Rees was actually the first of these adults I met, as he was the director of the Pride of Arizona marching band. While I didn't spend a lot of time with him one-on-one, I spent a lot of time on the field and in rehearsal with him over my four years at U of A. Although from the get-go he intimidated the heck out of me, it also was clear that he cared about his students. My parents came down for the first football game of my freshman year, and somehow they ended up introducing themselves to Rees. When they told him they were my parents, he knew who I was. This scared me a little as I was worried he might know who I was because I was messing up and would be able to call me out by name from the podium when I did. Eventually I realized it was actually evidence that he took the time to quickly get to know the names of the new students in the band at the beginning of every year, which impressed me when there was so much going on.

I learned a lot about leading a group from Rees. He pushed us and made us better by doing so. We literally would run drill sets countless times, stopping each time to evaluate what needed to be fixed and how that would get done. We would rehearse until 10:00 p.m. on a Friday night and be back on the field at 8:00 a.m. the next morning. When something didn't look good, or if we got lazy, he let us know, as he also did when something looked spot on. He also let us learn from watching ourselves. After each football game, we would watch the video of our pregame and halftime shows. Each week, we eagerly waited to see if the diagonals of the block "A" in the pregame hit or were off. The sets of the halftime show looked awesome, or they didn't. Without saying a word, Rees showed us what we needed to be ready to work on when we showed up for rehearsal on Monday. He expected us to work hard and to be dedicated, and he recognized when we were. During my senior year, I received a game ball, which was a great honor. Like on a sports team, each week the game ball went to someone who had been working especially hard and who set an example. We all wanted to receive a game ball at some point. It's still in my office now.

Marching band was a ton of work, but we were good, and we felt that. In high school, being in marching band made you a band geek. In college, being in the band impressed people. We were a part of something bigger than ourselves, and together we were something incredible. Band day was the culmination of all of our hard work, when we would perform a monolithic fifteen-minute, three-part show, leaving all of ourselves out on the field. In marching band, I learned how to kick my butt and to work hard in ways I physically had never done and under the desert sun. I experienced the rewards that came from this hard work, and I got to be a part of something bigger than me. Rees showed me what it was to lead people in this kind of endeavor.

Even though I was too intimidated to get to know Rees well, he was someone I knew was in my corner and I could turn to if I ever needed anything. He knew me through my actions, my showing up and working hard, day after day. Through watching him, I learned a ton, much of which I still use today.

Pastor Ben

During my first week of classes, I attended the BBQ for the PCM. They had just hired a new campus minister who I would meet about a month later when he started working at PCM, his first call out of seminary. Knowing that I, too, planned to go to seminary, this was an important relationship for me in multiple ways. First, Ben modeled campus ministry in much the way that I live it out now. He journeyed through college with us, helped us process our experiences, helped us to grow as leaders, and was just there through the ups and downs. Sometimes now, when I find myself wondering about something my students are doing, I pause and think back on my own college days, realizing that they are doing what I was doing. Then I wonder what that was like for Ben as I process how I feel about it in my role as the campus minister instead of the student!

Basically from the beginning, Ben gave me opportunities to learn and grow as I explored my calling to ministry. When I came to him with ideas for a book group, DVD discussion group, or mission trip to New Orleans post-Hurricane Katrina, he gave me the support to make them happen. I was able to get a lot of small group leadership experience during my time at PCM, which was great preparation for down the road! Beginning my sophomore year, I served as the student liaison on the board of directors, seeing the operational side of things and how Ben navigated working with the board. He took time to notice, name, and nurture the gifts for ministry he saw in me. He also would talk about how some day we would be colleagues, which we now are. It's nice to have this relationship where I can still call him and ask for advice, but we can also share the joys and challenges of our shared calling to ministry.

Ben did so much more than this though. He helped me grow in my faith, and he and his wife Gretchen helped me think about describing God more broadly, including through feminine language (I totally use Bobby McFerrin's feminine "Psalm 23 (Dedicated to My Mother)" with students now, which they first played for me. You can find it online if you want to listen for yourself). He gave me a great deal of spiritual and emotional support, listening to me ramble and go on about who knows how many different things over four years, always with patience and kindness. Whether I was crying about a guy or wanting to discuss some deep theological question, Ben was there for me.

Professor Swaim

I met Dr. Swaim the spring of my freshman year. She was a woman with incredible wisdom. She was seventy-one when I first took her class, and though she had traveled to over fifty countries, she also used Rumi to teach us that what we are looking for is normally not out there but within ourselves. She captured this in an email she sent me in September of my senior year regarding my senior thesis (which she was advising):

> I think you seem to be exploring your own curiosity, your own developing understanding of the basic questions of the human condition. The unknown has much greater fascination than the known (as in Whitman's poem about astronomy)! It is a fascination

which we share, so we will perhaps learn about ourselves at the same time.¹

She played a major role in my college experience that shows up throughout this book, so suffice it to say thank you here, and that from her I further learned the art of asking questions as a form of guidance and the beauty of being an avid lifelong learner.

Professor Marietta

I feel bad that the last paper I had to write in college was for Prof. Marietta because he did not deserve the last minute, this-is-all-that-stands-between-me-and-graduating-with-honors-and-I'm-ready-to-be-done piece of work. My apologies for that mediocre-at-best paper and thank you for your grace! I had Prof. Marietta for two classes during my senior year on Colonial and Revolutionary-era America. I have an interest in American history, but also enjoyed getting to know Dr. Marietta. He was also a Presbyterian and interested in hearing about the campus ministry. I visited him in office hours on occasion, and as a professor who knew me both academically and religiously, he was able to provide a reference for me that not all of my professors would have been able to. He also followed up to see how I was after I had moved on to seminary, which really meant something to me.

There is a story from the Old Testament that is a great example of mentoring, although it may be a bit of an unusual style of mentoring. The prophet Elijah chose a successor for himself, and as you can read above, did so in what may seem to us a peculiar fashion. Elisha was out in the fields one day, when this guy walks by and literally just throws his mantle, or cloak, over him. This act meant a great deal though; basically, he was saying, "Come, follow me." The mantle, a physical piece of clothing, is symbolic of so much more. The act of Elijah's is a reminder that sometimes we choose our mentors, and sometimes, our mentors choose us. God has a funny way of putting the people we need most in our lives just when we need them. Once they are in our lives, they deserve us putting time and effort into the relationship so they can continue to be important people in our lives for many years to

---

1. Prof. Swaim, email message to author, September 17, 2007. The poem she is referring to is Walt Whitman's "When I Heard the Learn'd Astronomer."

come. So Elijah throws his mantle on Elisha, and Elisha packs up and leaves home to go and follow this guy. For a long time, we don't hear anything else about Elisha and assume that he is following Elijah and learning from him as he observes and helps him in his work. When we next hear about Elisha, it's at a time when we learn that God is about to take Elijah up to heaven in a whirlwind. Elijah tells Elisha to stay behind, but Elisha refuses and stays by Elijah until the very end. When Elijah is taken, his mantle falls to the ground, and Elisha literally picks it up and carries it with him.

Sometimes, a mentor will literally pass on to you your life's work, but more often, they will help you discern your own calling and be a guide along your way. Depending on where you are in your college journey, you may or may not have had the time, or taken the time, to seek out these kinds of relationships. If you have not, it isn't too late, even if you're about to graduate this semester. If you have more time, find these adults whose mantles you want to carry, who you want to help shape and influence who you will become. Find people who will care about you, who you can talk to and tell about your victories and your setbacks, who will talk through big decisions with you.

One of the first steps in finding a mentor is finding someone who inspires you, someone you would love to talk more with about their field or their career or something they brought up in a lecture. If it's someone like your house dean (or whoever the adult in charge of your dorm is), it may just be that they seem like someone you could talk to about what's going on in your life. If something sparks you wanting to talk more to someone, listen to it. I know this can feel intimidating, but the worst thing that can happen if you reach out is they tell you they don't have the time. Most professors, staff, and chaplains like having students reach out though! Not only does it help us realize that students are indeed paying some attention to what we are doing, but engaging in the kinds of conversations this leads to is often thought provoking for the mentor as well.

Professors love to talk about their passions, and most professors want a student who wants to talk more about the subject. Don't always go by a professor's reputation either—a professor who has a reputation for being tough in the classroom may still be a great mentor! When seeking a mentor, or in a mentor–mentee relationship, it's important to still have some formal etiquette, such as giving them enough time to write a letter of recommendation if you ask them to (ideally at least two weeks; in order to write a good letter, they will need to find an hour or so to work on it). Writing these letters does take time, but it tends to be fun to get to brag about the students you work with and care for (though do think this through, if you put in a poor effort in a class, don't ask that professor for a letter of recommendation). As a woman, I also love empowering other young women to pursue their ambitions and try to support them along the way. It's also fun for me to hear students talk about mentoring younger students or high schoolers, helping pass on wisdom once again.

All of this said, there are plenty of stories of professors and mentors who have crossed a line and taken advantage of a student in one way or another. A mentor isn't worth crossing that line for, and you should move on from that person and protect yourself. I personally encountered sexism (thankfully not worse) from a professor that I wish I had reported to the Title IX office at our school. Several students have had professors they work for (such as in research assistant roles) ask unfair amounts of work from them (or work within an unfair deadline). Mentors can disappoint us in other ways too—we learn about something unethical they have done, they end up ghosting us at some point, they drop the ball on something we were relying on them for. Our mentors are human, and we all make mistakes. Sometimes the damage can be repaired, and sometimes it can't, which will always hurt. Sometimes, it ends up not the best fit anyways. Still, I have experienced things working out many more times than I have experienced them not working out.

Mentors stay with us, whether in real conversations or in how they have shaped us. While she was still alive, I went to visit Professor Swaim multiple times after college. I knew she would ask me the right questions to prod my thinking. I've kept in touch with Pastor Ben as well, now my colleague in ministry, and keep in touch with Prof. Rees on social media. The mantle we carry may end up looking more like a quilt, with pieces from many people, and I am grateful for them all.

Prayer

God of Wisdom,
Throughout Scripture, we see the knowledge
Of mentors and advisors passed on.
We thank you for the wise people
You have placed in our lives.
We give thanks for the teachers who shaped us when we were younger,
And those from other realms of our lives who

Helped us cultivate other interests and passions.
Guide us to those who have something to show us now,
Or who may benefit from our being in their life.
Open us to what they have to teach us,
About life, about ourselves, about faith,
Even about what it means to live well in this world.
Just as Elijah taught Elisha,
Allow us to learn from those whose mantles we will carry.
Amen.

REFLECTION QUESTIONS

1. Do you have relationships with any adults at college? If so, who are these adults? What made you interested in looking to them as a mentor?

2. If you were to draw a quilted mantle (either like a cloak or like a stole a pastor might wear), what would the sections of it look like? Who would they represent?

3. What is something in your life right now you could use a mentor to help you process?

4. You also can play a role for others as a mentor for them. Who might you mentor? How would that benefit them as well as yourself?

10

Loving Yourself

> Without loving ourselves, our other efforts to love fail.
>
> —Valerie Kaur

> Just because someone isn't willing or able to love us, it doesn't mean that we are unlovable.
>
> —Brené Brown

Scripture

But Mary stood weeping outside the tomb. As she wept, she bent over to look into the tomb; and she saw two angels in white, sitting where the body of Jesus had been lying, one at the head and the other at the feet. They said to her, "Woman, why are you weeping?" She said to them, "They have taken away my Lord, and I do not know where they have laid him." When she had said this, she turned around and saw Jesus standing there, but she did not know that it was Jesus. Jesus said to her, "Woman, why are you weeping? Whom are you looking for?" Supposing him to be the gardener, she said to him, "Sir, if you have carried him away, tell me where you have laid him, and I will take him away." Jesus said to her, "Mary!" She turned and said to him in Hebrew, "Rabbouni!" (which means Teacher). Jesus said to her, "Do not hold on to me, because I have not yet ascended to the Father. But go to my brothers and say to them, 'I am ascending to my Father and your Father, to my God and your God.'" Mary Magdalene went and announced to the disciples, "I have seen the Lord"; and she told them that he had said these things to her. (John 20:11–18)

ONE OF THE BOOKS I read while in college that helped me think about faith was Donald Miller's *Blue Like Jazz*. One of the things that has stuck with me from his book is his discussion of the commandment to "love your neighbor as you love yourself." While the commandment is often used to talk about loving others, we sometimes skip over the part where it says to do so only as we love ourselves. This means, first we have to love ourselves. Miller describes an epiphany he has and writes, "[God] was saying I would never talk to my neighbor the way I talked to myself, and that somehow I had come to believe it was wrong to kick other people around but it was okay to do it to myself."[1] For many of us who grew up in the church, the golden rule may have been one of the first Bible verses we learned: "Do to others as you would have them do to you" (Luke 6:31). If we want to talk about what it means to love others, both in friendships and in romantic relationships, we need to first talk about what it means to love ourselves.

One piece of this feels more straightforward than others, which is that college is a time when loving yourself means allowing yourself room to grow and learn about who you are. You have more space to explore who you are and what you believe when it comes to sex and sexuality. College is also a time when many students find themselves exploring their sexuality. For some, this started earlier than college, but for others, it is really once you have the freedom of being away from home that you begin to feel able to own who you are. One thing I have learned in my work and through my friendships is that no two stories look exactly the same, that everyone who identifies as LGBTQIA+ has had their own path to walk. For a number of students, something in college triggers a need to better explore their own identity. From what I've witnessed, this can be freeing and exciting, and also scary and sometimes painful as a student comes out first to themself and then maybe to friends or family, which can go well or horribly. For students coming from more conservative Christian backgrounds, there may be especially hurtful comments made, sometimes by people who believe they are speaking on behalf of God. Concerns about what their parents or loved ones might say mean that some students choose not to share this piece of themselves with their family, which for some makes going to visit

---

1. Miller, *Blue Like Jazz*, 306.

their families especially challenging. Students from this background often are already wrestling with their faith and if there is a place for someone like them in the church. There is, it just may not be in the churches and church communities you have experienced, but there are others out there flying the rainbow flag with pride and wanting to welcome you!

If you or a friend are figuring out your sexual identity and are a person of faith, find someone who can support you through this, especially if you come from a religious background that was unsupportive. Know that you are a beloved child of God exactly as you are, and that there are Christian denominations and churches that are welcoming and affirming of the queer community, who believe that God created each person exactly as we are and that no one needs to be fixed. Be gentle and kind to yourself if this is a journey you are on, and find others to support you when it gets tough. Enjoy living into who you are and be liberated in that self-knowledge.

During college, you also may find your own viewpoints around sex and sexuality may change too. Even though I grew up in a church where conversations around sex were more wholistic, Christian culture had still seeped into my life with its fairly conservative ideals. Over my time in school, I found my own thoughts changing, even though I wasn't really doing much dating. When I started college, I believed that sex was meant only for marriage, but by my senior year, my thoughts had changed. I'm not exactly sure what led them to change, other than maybe being better able to articulate that the quality of a relationship seemed to be more important to me than the legal status of the relationship (it was also influenced by taking a women's history course and becoming fed up with Victorian ideas and ideals forced onto women). This means my opinion changed, but I didn't all of a sudden think random hookups were a good idea (and by the way, there are far fewer of those happening than we are often led to believe). I don't think I would call casually hooking up sinful (and we'd need to define what is meant by this anyways), but I also believe it doesn't appreciate the fullness of relationship that we were created for. As our ideas change, it doesn't mean abandoning our faith. We need to wrestle with how our faith informs our thoughts around all of these topics. People will talk about sacred and secular realms, but the reality is that they are intertwined, one and the same. Sharing ourselves—mentally, emotionally, spiritually, and physically—with another person is a huge act of vulnerability, and not something we should treat lightly. What I learned as I grew is that this doesn't mean we have to throw up walls and barriers and rules, but it should lead us to be intentional, and to care about the wellbeing of both ourselves and others, including romantic partners. It asks us to be thoughtful, to let decisions be made by more than hormones, pressure, or fear, to articulate what you believe our faith has to say about our sexual choices, and hopefully act accordingly. Again, know that grace abounds.

One of the harder aspects of loving ourselves might be truly believing that we deserve to be loved. In talking to students about some of the struggles in college, one of the things that came up was what it feels like to be judged by others, especially based on physical appearances. They talked about how this is furthered by the whole concept of someone being in your league or out of your league, the idea that you aren't attractive enough for someone to want to date you, or that if they did, it wouldn't make sense because they could be dating someone who is more attractive. While my college experience didn't include the world of online dating, and Facebook was brand new, both dating apps and social media are part of the reality that you all encounter as you try to navigate this realm. Feeling like you have to compete with someone's carefully curated persona can make us feel like looking for someone to love us as we are is futile.

When students want to talk to me about a relationship, it's rarely because things are going the way they want them to be. Sure, when I'm catching up with a student who I know is in a relationship I'll ask how their partner is, how things are going, etc., but if a student specifically says they want to talk about their relationship, something is typically up. It might be something they are working through their thoughts about, such as that they are from a different faith tradition or an agnostic or atheist, trying to make sense of how their partner is impacted by their family systems, wondering what a future together might look like or something like these topics—good things to think about, but also things that many times can be worked through. Or it might be something more. Sometimes, they may be wondering if something is normal in a relationship, be concerned about if a relationship is unhealthy, or processing a relationship that was not healthy after it has ended.

Unfortunately, college is a time where a number of people experience an unhealthy or toxic relationship.[2] While there are typically not ways to

---

2. If you or a friend has experienced sexual violence, stalking, harassment, or something similar, your school should have staff members who are considered confidential resources who you can talk to about what has occurred. They can also provide help getting connected to any further resources you might want or need. An online search with your school's name and "confidential resources" should help you to find out who they are.

Loving Yourself

tell this before starting to get to know a person, and sometimes not until you are in a relationship, there are some things that if you notice you should pay attention to. This can be the case in both romantic relationships and platonic friendships. If you start to see things that feel strange or concerning, it is worth seeking out someone you trust and can talk to about this. Concerning behaviors can include when someone is trying to control your behavior or choices or isolating you from other friends. You might notice you feel drained by this person, lonelier when you are with them then when you are not, or that you feel like who you are is who they want you to be, not who you want to be. You may notice behavioral changes in yourself.

Pay attention to your body and to yourself. Often, our bodies and behaviors are revealing things going on subconsciously that we are just not aware of yet. Although it wasn't a toxic relationship, my body was once trying to let me know that the relationship I was in was causing me stress. During one semester of school, I noticed that I wasn't baking as much as I normally do, or as much as I like to do. I really enjoy baking, and I had tended to do so fairly often, even if it was just making cookies from a mix I bought at the store. I knew it was a busy semester. I had started dating someone right before the semester began. I was in my second year of an internship that I loved, but I had switched from going one day a week to two days, and with an hour drive each way that meant more time in the car getting to and from. There were also a few other things at my internship stressing me the first couple months. Plus, I had classes, work, etc. So when I noticed I wasn't baking that much, I attributed it to stress caused by all of these factors. Then, the stressful stuff at my internship got worked out and I still wasn't baking. While I thought I really liked the guy I was dating, as the semester unfolded it became more and more clear we were not a good match, and that the relationship was causing me a fair amount of stress. The day after I broke up with him, right before finals in December, I found myself making cookies. On the surface, I had thought if we could work through some things, the relationship might work, might get better, but deep inside, something knew that it wasn't right, and it was trying to tell me this. Pay attention to yourself and try to listen to what your body is telling you.

We should also pay attention if our friends are telling us they think something isn't quite right, as one of my friends was doing. This friend and I were on a flag football team together, and our team had made the championship game. He asked if my boyfriend was coming. I still remember the conversation and me saying, "No, he doesn't really like football," and my friend saying something very close to, "That doesn't matter. If he likes you, and this is something you care about, he should want to be there to support you." True, even if at the time I made a whole bunch of excuses as to why it was fine for him not to come. I felt like if he came to the game, I would have to spend time showing him I was grateful he came instead of having fun with my friends. In hindsight, I can see how all of this indicated that there was a bigger problem with the relationship. When your friends are telling you they see red flags, pay attention. They are likely able to see and articulate what you've become willing to accept.

When students come to talk to me about relationships that are not great relationships, part of what I hear is a deep longing to be accepted, a longing to be loved. It is fear that can drive people to stay connected to people they know are hurting them, be it a romantic partner or friend. I remember a student, I believe a sophomore at the time, who was telling me about sources of stress in their life, and it was clear that their relationship was a major source of stress. It sounded like it was unhealthy on both sides, with lots of unmet (and unrealistic) expectations that, when they weren't met, were followed by lots of yelling (again on both sides). It was the first real relationship the student talking with me had been in, and they were convinced they needed to make it work. Often, we seem to have this deep fear that if we leave this person, a romantic partner or friend, we worry it's possible no one will ever want to have the same kind of relationship with us ever again. We convince ourselves that it is better to have this broken, messed up relationship that we have than to take the risk to leave it and experience pain and loss, real loss. Though it is hard, leaving also opens up the possibility to find something so much better and healthier. Another challenge some students face after being sexually intimate with a partner for the first time may be a belief that they need to remain committed to that relationship, even if it doesn't feel like the right relationship. While there may be more for you to process coming out of this relationship, God wants you to have a good and fulfilling life, and that can mean leaving a relationship.

You deserve love that is real and good and true in both romantic and platonic relationships. Owning this is part of loving yourself and will allow you to love others better as well. Being loved for all of who you are, and being allowed to continue to grow and change, is part of what true love looks like.

Loving Yourself

I'm terrible with favorites; I have a half-dozen favorite anything, but this Scripture passage is one of my favorites. One of the things I love about it is that it hinges on the resurrected Jesus saying Mary's name. She hears her teacher, her friend, call her name, and that is how she recognizes him. I think about all that is caught up in that, what it feels like to have someone who truly knows and loves us say our name, what it feels like to feel known, to feel seen, in that way and in that moment. In this moment, her pain, grief, confusion, and hope, all feel acknowledged as Jesus speaks her name. When we can know, deep in our bones, that God loves us and calls us by name, then we can know we are known, seen, and loved in a way beyond all comprehension. We can truly love ourselves.

It's true that we are human and not God, and in this way, our love will never be perfect. We will make mistakes, hurt one another, and make choices that result in hurting ourselves too. We still are meant to love one another, but only as we love ourselves. May you, beloved child of God, know that you really and truly deserve to love yourself, and to be loved by others with a love that is good and true.

Prayer

Loving God,
We know we are supposed to love you,
And to love our neighbor,
But so often forget you also asked us
To do so as we love ourselves.
Help us to see ourselves how you see us,
With a gaze that is gentle and kind,
Full of compassion and pride.
When we wonder if we are lovable,
Remind us we are already loved.
Guide us to people
With whom we can have truly good relationships,
People who will love and care for our wellbeing,
As we care for theirs.
Thank you for loving us first,
So we might know love beyond our comprehension.
Amen.

You're Not the Only One

REFLECTION QUESTIONS

1. Have you thought about what it means to love you neighbor as yourself in the way Donald Miller talks about? How does it feel to think about it in this way?

2. What are some of the challenges you have found to loving yourself? If those are founded on myths, what might those myths be?

3. Have you ever experienced your body trying to tell you something? If so, what was that like? How did your body do so?

11

Loving Others

> The minute I heard my first love story,
> I started looking for you, not knowing
> how blind that was.
> Lovers don't finally meet somewhere,
> they're in each other all along.
>
> —Rumi

Love is giving up control. It's surrendering the desire to control the other person. The two—love and controlling power over the other person—are mutually exclusive. If we are serious about loving someone, we have to surrender all the desires within us to manipulate the relationship.

—Rob Bell

SCRIPTURE

Two are better than one, because they have a good reward for their toil. For if they fall, one will lift up the other; but woe to one who is alone and falls and does not have another to help. Again, if two lie together, they keep warm; but how can one keep warm alone? And though one might prevail against another, two will withstand one. A threefold cord is not quickly broken. (Eccl 4:9–12)

Set me as a seal upon your heart,
as a seal upon your arm,

> for love is strong as death,
> passion fierce as the grave.
> Its flashes are flashes of fire,
> a raging flame.
> Many waters cannot quench love,
> neither can floods drown it.
> If one offered for love
> all the wealth of one's house,
> it would be utterly scorned.
> (Song 8:6–7)

LET'S ALSO EXPLORE WHAT it means to love others, both romantically and otherwise, but in close, personal relationships. One of the fun things about Disney's *Frozen* was that Disney decided to poke fun at the whole concept of the whirlwind movie romance, which many of their movies have been based upon. In the course of a two-minute song, young Anna goes from having her first real interaction with Hans to accepting his proposal. Turns out (spoiler alert!), Prince Charming isn't actually all that charming, but the youngest of thirteen brothers and is only trying to use Anna to get his own throne. Before that realization, the song "Love Is an Open Door" captures what many of us long for: meeting someone and suddenly knowing that this is the person you will spend happily-ever-after with while you finish each other's sandwiches. And it's not just Hollywood that has given us these messages. Students have shared with me that during the freshman orientation at Penn, one of the things they are told is that your future spouse may be sitting in this room. For a few, including some students I've worked with, this is true, but for most of us that won't be the case, and at eighteen, that idea can feel a little overwhelming.

The love story I grew up with, the one I thought my life would resemble, was my parent's love story. I imagine many of us probably do this; we look to what we know. Even for those whose parents separated or divorced when you were young, there is probably a greater fear that this will be more possible for you. My parents met when my dad was working on his master's degree and my mom was a senior in college. They were introduced in passing by their boss in December, had their first real conversation in January, went on their first date the day before Valentine's Day, got engaged at the end of March, and married in August. I always assumed that I likewise would be engaged by the end of college, though maybe to someone I had known a little bit longer than the six weeks my parents had known each other when they got engaged. Such was not the case for me. In fact, I didn't have a relationship between my senior year of high school and the summer after I graduated college. Let's just say that it was still an emotional roller coaster. Some days I wondered what was wrong with me and why I was perpetually single, and others I loved and embraced the freedom and independence of not being attached to a significant other.

Marriage has shifted to occurring later these days, but we may still go into college dreaming we'll meet "the one" while in school and fall wildly in love. While it ultimately worked for my parents (they've been married for over four decades), they both went through ugly, painful breakups in college before meeting each other. College is a time of growth, and that can take many different forms. College is a time where, as with many other aspects of your life, you have the opportunity to explore what it is you are looking for when it comes to relationships. You might explore what you are looking for in a partner, which we often do by dating. I know this may sound funny given that we often end up in relationships that started after hanging out leads to being a couple over time and so you never really went on any dates and quite frankly you maybe never even really defined your relationship, but you can learn a lot on an actual date. Maybe it's fantastic and you can't wait to go on another date, or maybe the person only talks about themselves the whole time and you realize they are more into themselves than they are into you, or maybe they articulate a worldview that is completely incompatible with your own. You realize you want a partner with more of a sense of adventure, who is more or less serious, who has a more compatible sense of humor, all different kinds of things. A friend described a date in which they went on a nature walk as being a metaphor for the potential future of the relationship—whenever they came to a fork, they both went for different paths, and she took this to mean they were looking for different things in life (don't worry, that was based off of their conversation and not just their choice of path, it was just the metaphor). Going on a date is both exciting and scary, putting ourselves out there always involves a risk (and it is important to make sure we do so as safely as possible). It also provides us with a chance to learn so much about ourselves and others, and perhaps the chance to start a relationship with someone who will bring happiness into your life and make you an even better person.

Everything I've talked about so far has emotional elements, and all of this can result in heartbreak and heartache, including being single! I remember one day I met with Pastor Ben and sat on his couch just crying.

I don't remember when exactly in college this was, but I do remember, at least in part, what and who it was about. It was about the fact that, at least from my perspective, I had plenty of great guy friends in my life, none of whom seemed to be interested in more than friendship with me. Some days I was okay with this reality, other days, like this day, I despaired. This is a way I have felt many times about my life when it comes to love and relationships, and when I do, it often leads to a pity party (especially when I was younger). I've also come to realize it's probably a pretty skewed reality. It's possible that some of these guys were actually interested in me, but I never took the risk to find out. It's also probable that there have been guys I never gave the time of day to, who may have been quite interested in me. And yes, there have been those who I wasn't interested in but were interested in me, a sometimes flattering though often painful experience in and of itself. It is hard to know you are causing someone else pain, even when you know it's the right path forward.

I've been talking about romantic relationships, but those aren't the only relationships we should be seeking. The passage from Ecclesiastes is a beautiful passage, often read at weddings, but not inherently talking about lovers. It's talking about companionship. While love and romance is an important aspect of life, it cannot be our only source of strength and relationship. One of the courses I took in college was on women's history in the US from the colonial era until the early twentieth century. It's actually one of the courses I remember the most from and helped shape and develop my thoughts around female sexuality (and for that matter, practices around childbirth). One of the lectures I remember was on some mid- to late nineteenth-century letters that women wrote to each other. At first glance, they may seem like love letters, but many scholars don't feel that they are actually homoerotic. These letters between female friends, express longing to be with each other, address physical though not expressly sexual touch, and speak of the jealousy experienced when a female friend would marry and now have a husband requiring her time and attention. For some of these women, their marriage was more practical than anything. Their husband provided an income and a way to create children, but their emotional support came from their female friends.

Today, our culture puts so much emphasis on romantic relationships, on finding your other half, the person who will make you happy and whole. There is a sense that once you find this person, everything is just happily-ever-after, which I know from many of my happily married friends is not at all how it actually plays out. While there is a lot that we can find and gain from being in love with someone, we cannot rely on that romantic relationship to provide us everything in life. Somewhere between the extremes of finding the person who will make your life complete and a marriage that is strictly for practical purposes like some of those nineteenth-century ones is a middle ground where a healthy romance and healthy friendships create a wonderful community in which we can thrive or where you lead a single but fulfilling life because you still have companionship. If you are in a relationship, it is also important to maintain friendships that aren't wrapped up in the relationship, both just to have in general and to help support you in the event the relationship does end. These may include friendships, strictly friendships, with people of the gender(s) that you are also attracted to. This does not preclude us from having platonic relationships, even if you have heard or been told otherwise (I have seen this most around male–female friendships but have also heard it used outside these constraints as well). The experience of developing long-term friendships is something you'll continue to learn how to do in college, and hopefully, whether or not you meet your spouse, you do meet some lifelong companions at school.

The first time I took a course called Spirituality in the Arts with Dr. Swaim, the course was based around Jewish philosopher Martin Buber's 1923 work *I and Thou*. This beautiful work explores the nature of relationships and the ways we connect with one another, which is what we spent the semester exploring in the class. Buber puts forth two types of ways that we connect with another. Most of the time, we function in "I-It" relationships. Whenever we put any kind of label, or identity, onto another person or onto ourselves, they functionally become an "it." This includes gender, age, race, relationship to me, etc. When we apply this label, we have made them into a thing. "I-Thou" connections tend to be mere moments within relationships that often function in "I-it mode." These are moments where these labels are transcended, and you connect soul to soul. Nothing gets in the way; you no longer are distanced by the divisions we create.[1] In this class, we read Yann Martel's novel *Life of Pi* and discussed if it's possible to have an "I-Thou" relationship with an animal. We walked a labyrinth as we explored what it means to have an "I-Thou" relationship with ourselves. This class is also where I was introduced to the Sufi mystic poet Rumi, who described an "I-Thou" relationship in this way:

> Out beyond ideas of right-doing and wrong-doing,

1. Buber, *I and Thou*, 53–85.

there is a field. I'll meet you there.
When the soul lies down in that grass,
the world is too full to talk about.
Ideas, language, even the phrase each other
doesn't make any sense.[2]

You have to sit with Rumi's writings and let them sink in, but these soul-to-soul moments, these I and Thou moments, are glimpses of the divine that we need in our lives. They can never be forced, but we can open ourselves up to them, and sometimes they occur where we least expect them.

Who knows what your college time will look like when it comes to dating. Maybe you'll be in a long-term relationship (or several), maybe you'll go on lots of first dates, maybe you won't date at all. One thing I firmly believe is that we were created to live in community, and that we need companions on our journey. In my high school youth group, when we circled up to pray, we would all put our thumbs to the left, so we had one hand to support the hand in ours, and one hand being supported by the hand under ours. As the passage from Ecclesiastes says, it's better when we are together so we can help each other up, but honestly, I enjoy life more when I share it with other people (as long as I get my introvert time as well!). At the end, the passage talks about the threefold cord, often seen as bringing God into the relationship. My lasting relationships from college are the ones that did just that.

Prayer

God of love,
You created us as beings who desire intimacy,
Yet we are vulnerable,
Our hearts easily broken,
And we are young,
Wanting to make our own way in the world.
Help us to navigate through the world of romance
In ways that are authentic to ourselves
And that allow us to grow as well.
Let us use this time at college,
Where we are learning and growing in so many ways,
To learn about this side of ourselves too,

---

2. Rumi, *Open Secret*, 8.

Who we really are,
And what we might seek in a partner.
Help us not forget that we also need companions,
People who we can support and who will support us,
And help us up when we fall.
Keep us open in all of these relationships and others,
For the moments of soul to soul encounters,
When we may glimpse you.
Amen.

Reflection Questions

1. Had you thought about what you expected college to be like in terms of dating? If so, what did you expect? What has your actual experience been like?
2. What do you think are some of the benefits and costs of dating?
3. What do you think companionship brings to our lives? Why does having companions matter?
4. Have you ever had an "I-Thou" experience? What was that like?

12

What Should I Do with My Life?

> The place God calls you to is the place where your deep gladness and the world's deep hunger meet.
>
> —Frederick Buechner

> All I'm saying is simply this: that all [hu]mankind is tied together; all life is interrelated, and we are all caught in an inescapable network of mutuality, tied in a single garment of destiny. Whatever affects one directly, affects all indirectly. For some strange reason I can never be what I ought to be until you are what you ought to be. And you can never be what you ought to be until I am what I ought to be—this is the interrelated structure of reality.
>
> —Martin Luther King Jr.

> There is no life without a task; no person without a talent; no place without a fragment of God's light waiting to be discovered and redeemed; no situation without its possibility of sanctification; no moment without its call. It may take a lifetime to learn how to find these things, but once we learn, we realize in retrospect that all it ever took was the ability to listen. When God calls, he[1] does not do so by way of universal imperatives. Instead, he whispers our name—and the greatest reply, the reply of Abraham, is simply hineni: "Here I am," ready to heed your call, to mend a fragment of your all-too-broken world.
>
> —Rabbi Jonathan Sacks

---

1. You'll notice throughout the book that I try to use gender-neutral language when referring to God. Where masculine language remains, it is because it is in the author's original quote or in the translation of Scripture being used.

What Should I Do with My Life?

Do your little bit of good where you are; it's those little bits of good put together that overwhelm the world.

—Archbishop Desmond Tutu

Scripture

Now the word of the Lord came to me saying,
"Before I formed you in the womb I knew you,
and before you were born I consecrated you;
I appointed you a prophet to the nations."
Then I said, "Ah, Lord God! Truly I do not know how to speak, for I am only a boy." But the Lord said to me,
"Do not say, 'I am only a boy';
for you shall go to all to whom I send you,
and you shall speak whatever I command you.
Do not be afraid of them,
for I am with you to deliver you,
says the Lord."
Then the Lord put out his hand and touched my mouth; and the Lord said to me,
"Now I have put my words in your mouth.
See, today I appoint you over nations and over kingdoms,
to pluck up and to pull down,
to destroy and to overthrow,
to build and to plant."
(Jer 1:4–10)

I'M ONE OF THOSE unusual people who have known what they were going to do careerwise for a long time, at least to some extent. After a stint of wanting to be a wildlife photographer in late elementary school (which I still think sounds awesome), by sometime around eighth grade I knew I was going to become a pastor. There was no moment of sudden clarity, no lightning bolt or burning bush. I don't even remember what first drew me towards it. A friend recently shared that she remembers it being well before eighth grade I knew I wanted to be a pastor, and I imagine she's right. What I remember is that I had the deep sense that this is what I was supposed to do with my life, a sense that I could not ignore. I loved reading and writing, and I remember adults commenting on my gifts for writing during middle school when I wrote a couple pieces for the youth and church newsletters. Although no one was telling me specifically that this was what I was supposed to do with my life, this sense of what I felt called to do was affirmed by others.

When I told people what I wanted to be (especially adults), I never remember anyone expressing surprise (my high school peers at school were a different story). When people ask now about my feeling called to ministry at a young age, I sometimes say that I think it was God's way of dealing with my stubbornness by just preempting it entirely. I sometimes wonder what would have happened if I hadn't listened to this call until later on, after I had created a different life plan. Would I have fought it, as my stubbornness can lead me to do. Would it have taken me years to listen? What made me hear God's call in the first place? As I thought about going to college, I decided that I didn't want to study religion for seven years straight, and if I needed a backup career, I thought maybe I could be a high school English teacher (I've since been informed by my mother and sister, having edited papers they each wrote, that I might make too many students cry with my paper editing). So, I became an English major, which let me study other things that I enjoyed as well as develop the critical reading and writing skills that would prepare me for seminary.

We use this weird language in the church—"discernment," "call," and "vocation" (which comes from the Latin *vocare*, meaning "to call")—often without stopping to take some time to explore what these terms mean. Let's step back for a moment and look at what this whole vocation or call thing even means. In many ways it is hard to describe, but it might best be described as this deep, abiding sense that there is something you are supposed to do—with your afternoon, during a period of time, or with your life. Since that still is fairly vague, maybe you've seen Disney's *Moana*. While this movie is in part a coming-of-age story, it is also a story about call, about vocational discernment, about Moana learning who she is meant to be. For Moana, it is about her learning about her cultural heritage and the Polynesian wayfinding traditions. While it may lack explicit Christian language, there is much we can learn from it as each of us seek to find our way.

Moana, we learn, has been drawn to the water since she was able to walk. Her community lives on an island, but they now only go out to fish in boats that stay close to the shore. As we meet the teenage Moana, she sings about being pulled by the horizon. When we talk about call, part of what we are talking about is what is pulling Moana to the ocean's horizon, a sense deep inside that this is part of you and where you belong. As she sings this, internally she is wrestling with belonging to her people who refuse to sail out on the ocean and her future role as their leader. Much later in the movie, she realizes that "The call isn't out there at all, it's inside me" and always has been.[2]

As you think about where or what you may be called to, some things to consider are your gifts, talents, passions, and experiences. If there are people who can tell you about you as a toddler, ask them what you were like, what held your attention, what kind of activities you were drawn towards. For many of us, our adult selves are really quite similar to who we were as children. We now express it in different ways, and sometimes lose touch with parts of ourselves along the way, often thinking they were childish. The reality is that there are often deep truths about who we are that have presented themselves in one way or another since we were young.

One of my favorite things about Moana's journey of discernment is the role her grandmother plays. Her grandmother sees who Moana might become from her infancy and helps Moana to see it. We need outside voices to help us live into the people God calls each of us to be, and often to help us discern what the work God is calling us to might look like. Moana's grandmother brings a life full of experience, and is comfortable in her own skin even if, she says, the village thinks she is "the village crazy lady."[3] Before Moana begins her journey, her grandmother tells Moana that the voice inside is who she is. While this is an important and powerful moment, the bigger moment for me is when her grandmother's spirit comes to her at a critical moment on her journey. Her grandmother truly sees Moana and who she has become and acknowledges this, as well as the hardships she has encountered, the scars—physical, mental, emotional, and spiritual—that have shaped her into the person she is now. She says to Moana,

> The people you love will change you
> The things you have learned will guide you
> And nothing on Earth can silence
> The quiet voice still inside you
> And when that voice starts to whisper
> Moana, you've come so far
> Moana, listen

---

2. Musker and Clements, *Moana*, 1:21:35.
3. Musker and Clements, *Moana*, 21:10.

You're Not the Only One

Do you know who you are?[4]

In this moment, Moana claims who she is, and in doing so claims the call to complete her voyage. In multiple ways, we need people in our own lives to play roles similar to the role Moana's grandmother plays. We need family, friends, mentors, and communities who watch us grow. Sometimes these people are the ones who notice what makes us come alive, what sparks our passions. They can notice our gifts and talents, and feed that back to us. They can help us through times of trial, when the path gets rocky and challenging. Some have taken the path before us and can help point us in the right direction when we get lost. These people play critical roles and can help keep us from chasing after something we may not really be called to. My sister sometimes tells our mother that she is squashing her dreams, but sometimes, what may feel like that may actually be someone pointing us toward a dream we were created for.

In his book *Let Your Life Speak: Listening for the Voice of Vocation*, Parker Palmer talks about "way opening" and "way closing," and the role each can play in our discernment.[5] When a way closes, it can be painful, but also directive. Maybe you had planned to major in a certain subject, but you can't stand one of the required courses. Maybe you don't get an internship or a job you had wanted. A way has closed, but maybe another way is opening. Our plans can change, by choice or by reality. While I knew what I wanted to do when I started college, my sister had several ideas, and I think had five different majors during college, though she didn't get through the process of declaring each of them. She still didn't know what she wanted to do when she finished college. This has been true for a number of my friends, and a number of students I worked with. There is no timeline for this journey, and each of our journey's will look different from our friends and peers in one way or another. Even when the way forward may not seem clear, God will use all of your experiences and what you have learned from them wherever you end up.

It's also important to remember that what God calls you to, along with your vocation, is not just your job. In fact, it is not even a singular thing. Vocation is about how we live and what we do with our entire life. Being a son or daughter, a sibling, a friend, a roommate, a mentor, and someday maybe a spouse or parent is part of our vocation. Currently, being a student

---

4. Musker and Clements, *Moana*, 1:20:23.
5. Palmer, *Let Your Life Speak*, 37–55.

is part of your vocation. Using your gifts and talents to serve the world, through a career or through volunteering, is part of your vocation. God has called us to be disciples, to help make our world look more like the one God envisions, and we each have gifts that help us discern how we might go about doing this. Part of what can happen in this season of your life is developing a better understanding of your gifts and talents. Sometimes we know what they are, and sometimes others help us figure them out. It could be a family member or mentor remarking on how gifted you seem at something or noticing your passion around a certain issue or activity. It could be a question someone asks, such as, "Have you ever thought about doing X?" God can speak to us in a huge variety of ways.

While this may seem hard to believe while you are in college, when it would really feel nice to have it all figured out, the truth is that you don't have to have your whole life figured out. When I graduated college and started seminary, I didn't think I was going to become a campus minister. Several things changed over the course of my time at seminary. First, I quickly discovered that my passion was for practical theology, and so I switched into a dual degree program, adding another year to my education. This is one of the best decisions I made. While there were many classes I enjoyed, the practical theology classes were almost guaranteed to be life-giving for me, to help me take what I was learning in other classes and turn it into something that felt usable. I've seen a similar discovery in one of the students involved with the CA, who found his classes almost a chore but asked for books on economics for Christmas and loved reading them. During the summer between his sophomore and junior year, he realized he could change his major to economics and study something he was interested in, and that was exciting to him. It gave him a path to follow that energized him.

Even after I switched into the dual degree, I still thought I was headed to work in the church until I felt God changing things up my third year, leading to a realization that where I had always planned on going next may not be where I was headed. I decided to do an internship in campus ministry my last year in school and felt like I could see myself there, and so I applied for campus ministry jobs. Now that I'm here, there are lots of pieces I can see coming together that have led me to this place, but it's only in hindsight that we get that clarity. When I consider where I have ended up, I kind of laugh because while I didn't expect to be in campus ministry until it happened, it fits. When I was young, both of my parents worked in higher education at a community college; my mom as a career counselor (which I feel like I do a decent amount of as a campus minister) and my dad worked in admissions (access and retention have always been very important to him). My dad shifted in higher education to software system development and then consulting, but with those same concerns remaining central for him. My mom moved to working in the church when I was ten years old. So blending the church and higher education seems a quite natural progression for me to have taken, despite my adamant refusal to apply to the University of Kansas, their alma mater, because I wanted to forge my own path (I told you, I can be stubborn). We also see in *Moana* the role that our ancestors play in shaping who we are, both those living and those who have already passed on. Her ancestors were voyagers, and now, she has learned, so is she.

Another call story that has often resonated with me is Jeremiah's story, in part because of his excuse of being young when he is called to be a prophet. It was read at my ordination service. It also gives me pause because it reminds me of the weight of what God will ask us to do. Jeremiah is called to do some stuff that won't be met with a generally positive response, but he is proclaiming what the people needed to hear. It is a reminder that God promises to go with us wherever we may be called to go and equips us for the journey, either through what we ourselves can do or through those who go with us.

I get you may be frustrated that this chapter didn't tell you how to figure out what to do with your life in step-by-step instructions. I think that is how some of the students have felt when we come back from the CA's vocational discernment retreat we've had some years. It's not meant to be something you figure out over a weekend or by reading a chapter. Hopefully, some of the things in this chapter have sparked something for you, something to further explore or contemplate, but this is also a lifelong journey. Yes, I consider my work as a minister my call, but I also think I'm called to respond to that feeling that one of my friends could really use a phone call just to see how they are doing. The vocation of being a disciple of Jesus means constantly listening for what God might be calling us to today and throughout our lives!

PRAYER

Speaking God,
Help us to listen and to hear

What Should I Do with My Life?

What you are saying to us.
Give us the wisdom to discern what it is
You are calling us to,
Today, tomorrow, and every day.
Help us to see our vocations,
Not just a career,
But as a family member or friend,
a citizen, even as a friendly customer in the checkout line.
Show us how our gifts and passions
Can help this world look more like the one
That you have promised us will be,
The kingdom Jesus talked so much of.
Amen.

Reflection Questions

1. In *Moana*, Maui has tattoos that tell the story of his life and depict events that explain what has made him into the person he is. Take some time to draw what your tattoos would be.

2. Do you know what you want to do careerwise? If so, what makes that what you want to do, and what makes you a good fit for that? How does it connect to your faith? If you don't know what you want to do, what thoughts do you have based off your interests and talents?

3. What are some of the things God might call us to each and every day? Where do you "hear" God speaking to you, and do you have intentional practices to create more of the kind of space where you can listen to and for God?

13

When God Calls You to Go to Unexpected Places or Do Unexpected Things

In response to God's call, Moses quickly comes up with five objections: 1) "Who am I?" 2) "Who are you?" 3) "What if they do not believe me?" 4) "I stutter." 5) "Why not send someone else?" If it were not the classic biblical text, I would assume this exchange to be a cartoon in the *New Yorker*! In each case, God stays in the dialogue, answering Moses respectfully and even intimately, offering a promise of personal Presence and an ever-sustaining glimpse into who God is—Being Itself, Existence Itself, a nameless God beyond all names, a formless God previous to all forms, a liberator God who is utterly liberated. God asserts God's ultimate freedom from human attempts to capture God in concepts and words by saying, "I am who I am" (Exodus 3:14). Over the course of his story we see that Moses slowly absorbs this same daring freedom.

—Richard Rohr

Scripture

Now the boy Samuel was ministering to the Lord under Eli. The word of the Lord was rare in those days; visions were not widespread. At that time Eli, whose eyesight had begun to grow dim so that he could not see, was lying down in his room; the lamp of God had not yet gone out, and Samuel was lying down in the temple of the Lord, where the ark of God was. Then the Lord called, "Samuel! Samuel!" and he said, "Here I am!" and ran to Eli, and said, "Here I am, for you called me." But he said, "I did not call;

When God Calls You to Go to Unexpected Places

lie down again." So he went and lay down. The Lord called again, "Samuel!" Samuel got up and went to Eli, and said, "Here I am, for you called me." But he said, "I did not call, my son; lie down again." Now Samuel did not yet know the Lord, and the word of the Lord had not yet been revealed to him. The Lord called Samuel again, a third time. And he got up and went to Eli, and said, "Here I am, for you called me." Then Eli perceived that the Lord was calling the boy. Therefore Eli said to Samuel, "Go, lie down; and if he calls you, you shall say, 'Speak, Lord, for your servant is listening.'" So Samuel went and lay down in his place. Now the Lord came and stood there, calling as before, "Samuel! Samuel!" And Samuel said, "Speak, for your servant is listening." (1 Sam 3:1–10)

WORK WITH ME HERE because the following story is a little tricky to tell. During the spring of my freshman year, I remember starting to feel what I thought was a somewhat odd stirring, a call to do something. I felt called to go and serve in Africa. I realize that sounds somewhat ignorant, and yes, even as this happened, I knew that Africa was a large continent made up of many individual countries and this was going to need to be a little more specific. I also was aware of, and not wanting to further, the white savior complex[1] that white Christians have been guilty of individually and corporately in so many ways. The whole thing seemed pretty odd to me, as I had never felt any kind of strong pull to travel to somewhere in Africa before, so I wondered what was going on. After about three weeks passed and the feeling did not go away, I told my mom about it, expecting her to be like, "Okay, maybe that will be something you can do down the road, you're young, and the right opportunity will come." I did not expect what she said instead, which was, "Figure it out and we'll go." What? That was not what I anticipated, but over the next few months we began to organize a college-aged opportunity to spend three weeks in Kenya the following summer, where we would visit, learn about, and work with several churches and organizations that Mt. View, my home church, had supported and been in relationship with for many years.

So, fifteen months after I first felt this call, I boarded a plane with my mom and six other college-aged women. While we were there, since it made sense to plan the trips together, an adult group from Mt. View also

---

1. This is the idea that white people can "save" others, specifically people of color and often those with less economic means, by bringing them resources, enlightenment, etc., that they believe these other people need and cannot acquire on their own.

came to Kenya to visit the same places and also form and further personal relationships with the organizations we already financially supported. In the years since, multiple groups have gone back, and many relationships have been formed, relationships that have changed lives here in the United States and in Kenya. The relationships were by far the most important thing to come out of both the college and adult trips. During my time in Kenya, I learned just how culturally significant relationships are to the people of Kenya, which is something we in the United States could learn a lot from.

One of the things that fascinates me about the whole experience is that, even by the time the trip finished, I felt God was using me as a tool, a way to get something bigger into motion. I had a wonderful experience and am grateful for the time I spent in Kenya and the people I got to meet. Ultimately, I felt like my role was to get a ball in motion, and that this trip was really not about my experience, but about the experience others had and about rekindling relationships between our congregation and the congregation and organizations we spent time with in Kenya. God could have made this happen in plenty of different ways, and had I not responded probably still would have, yet this happened because I had called my mom about a weird feeling I had, and the way was made clear. It made me realize how God really does use us as part of the bigger story, and that we need to listen when we sense that God is calling us to do something, even when that something seems very unexpected and even improbable.

This passage that tells the story of Samuel is one that always makes me smile because it highlights for me how difficult it can be for us to not just hear but to recognize when God is talking to us. It shows us how easily we can confuse God's voice with the noise of our lives, and how we often need help distinguishing it. Samuel, still young, hears a voice, hears someone calling him, and since he and Eli are the only people around, assumes it's Eli calling him. I imagine Samuel going in and waking Eli, and Eli, half asleep, being like, "Go back to bed! I didn't call you." Then it happens again (annoying), then it happens a third time (ok, what's going on here?). At this point, Eli, who has heard God's voice in his life, realizes what is occurring and tells Samuel to go back to bed, and when he hears the voice calling him again, to respond and to listen. It's an example not just of learning how to listen for and respond to God, but of mentorship and guidance. Eli plays an important roll in this story because when God calls us to do the expected or unexpected, we need someone who is a little wiser than we are to help us know what steps to take, to help us discern if this seems legitimate or something of our own creation. Not every voice we hear in the middle of the night belongs to God (for me, the middle of the night can sometimes be a very dark, dangerous place to be alone with my thoughts), and it is good to have companions who can help us determine what it is we are hearing or to be the ones delivering the message.

Ironically, one of my personal examples of God calling me to do something and using others to help me get that message is the writing of this book. Before seminary, I never had any interest in getting a PhD, but as I met the practical theology PhD students, and saw what that looked like, I couldn't help but wonder if it was something I wanted to do. As I settled into life as a campus minister at the CA, I struggled with not knowing what was next. I had always had a next step until this point—college, then seminary, then finding a call (the place I would be a pastor to). I continued to wrestle with whether I should pursue a PhD. Even while I talked about it as a possibility, I knew something about it didn't feel right. I am the kind of person who tends to go after what I want (sometimes for better or for worse). Why was I not researching programs or studying to take the GRE (which I didn't have to take for seminary)? I knew I needed to listen to what my inaction was telling me but felt unsure what that meant. I can still picture the two incidents that happened next.

In the late winter of 2015, a student who had started coming to the CA a few weeks prior and I were talking in the basement one day when she said she wanted to read my book. I laughed and said that I hadn't written a book, so there was nothing for her to read, and life moved on. A couple months later (it had warmed up enough to be eating outside), I got lunch with a student the chaplain's office had connected me to, a student I met for the first time as we sat down to eat. At some point in the conversation, she said the same exact words: "I want to read your book." I said the same thing—there is no book—but the message had gotten through with a bit of a hit over the head (I mean, the second time seemed a bit of a glowing sign). I started toying with the idea of writing a book and realized that this idea felt like it "fit" so much better than pursuing a PhD, at least in this stage of my life. It made me excited, made me want to get to work. While it has been a slow, decade-long process, it still feels like what I am supposed to be doing (I think), and once it's done, I have absolutely no idea what God will show me is next!

What may seem unexpected may not actually be that surprising in many cases, once we are able to see it with a wider perspective and within a broader context. I have often found that one of my roles in many situations seems to be a bridge builder or connector, connecting people to each other or to resources, organizations, etc. This is the exact role I played in the trip to Kenya, so my being the conduit made sense in hindsight. With regards to this book, one of the first gifts I remember adults naming was my writing. Although I continued to write academic papers in college and seminary, and sermons after, it had been over a decade since I had seriously spent time writing what I would call spiritually reflective writing, and I needed to find that part of me again. When you feel called to do something that may seem unexpected, there is something that you likely already possess, a skill or talent that is underlying the call, and it may only be later that you see how the pieces all fit together.

While one of the unexpected places God called me to in college was thousands of miles away across an ocean on a different continent, the strange place can just as likely be a room down the hall from yours. A gentle nudge to go introduce yourself to someone in your dorm or in your class, someone who may seem quite different than you, could lead to an incredible friendship. Maybe you'll decide to switch your major and study something completely different from that path you had imagined, something that makes you feel alive and that you get excited just talking to others about. It could mean pursuing a career others might be surprised by, not because it doesn't fit you but because it doesn't fit the expectations of others. I see this with some of the students I've worked with who go on to careers like teaching, ministry, social work, etc., whose peers and sometimes families are surprised they wouldn't pursue more financially lucrative careers.

Talking about listening for God always sounds a little crazy to me because while I have definitely received messages I would say are from God and have felt God leading me to do certain things in and with my life, I have never heard a "God voice" spelling something out for me. Sometimes I feel a sense I should do something and wonder if that's God, just random neurons firing, or my stomach growling. This is why I rely so much on trusted people in my life to help sort it all out, and why I always feel privileged to get to play that role for students and alumni of the CA. It's amazing how much somebody tells you when they talk to you, both through what they say and what they don't say and by how their body reveals more than what their words alone do—when they relax and get excited, when they pull in and become a little more on guard. The more in touch we are with our bodies, the more we can listen to what they reveal to us, which can reveal what is happening in our subconscious.

Another thing I think about is fear and the roll that fear plays when God calls us to do the unexpected. How do we figure out when to push through the fear and when to let it make us pause and maybe reevaluate the situation? Honestly, I don't think I have a set answer. Sometimes the same people who are those I talk through things with, who help me discern, are the ones who feel the most concerned when I go to do something that has an element of risk to it. Sometimes those are the people who have a plan for your life that looks quite different from the one that you end up feeling called to live. Fear, ours or others, can lead us to want to make excuses like the ones Richard Rohr talks about Moses making when God called him to go lead the Israelites out of captivity.[2] I definitely have made my own excuses before—not having time probably being the most frequent one, along with not being skilled enough—and I imagine you have your own. Ultimately, we will find the greatest fulfillment when we follow where God is leading us.

All of this said, following God in a faithful life of discipleship, including the times when you are called to do something that wasn't in the plan, is more of an art than a science. The unknown always has an element of fear to it, even when it is also exciting, which should help us remember to rely on God to see us through. The experience of hearing God was new, foreign, to Samuel. When Moses was called to do both the unexpected and the improbable, Moses had questions and excuses ready for God. Neither one made their journey alone, and both had their lives transformed by following where God led. When we follow God to unexpected places, our lives and others can be transformed too.

PRAYER

God of surprises,
Sometimes you call us to places
We never expected to find ourselves.
This might be a physical place,
A spiritual or emotional one,
A new sense of self,
That utilizes some of our core gifts.

---

2. Rohr, *Soul Brothers*, 17–19.

Wherever it is you call us,
You are already there,
And will be with us through the journey.
Guide us to those who will be our Elis,
Those who will help us discern when we are hearing your voice,
And know how to respond,
"Speak Lord, I am listening."
Help us trust in you,
When we step out feeling uncertain but with faith.
Amen.

Reflection Questions

1. Have you experienced God's call in your life? If so, what has this looked like? If not, what do you think it might look like? Have you followed God's call without realizing that's what it was?

2. Who are the Elis in your life? How do they help you discern what is going on or help you hear God's voice? What are some of the ways you can play this role for others?

3. What are some of the challenges of following God when you are called to do things that you hadn't seen as part of the plan for your life? What might these challenges require of you? How can you work through them?

14

How Am I Going to Get It All Done? (Insert Panic Here)

> To achieve great things, two things are needed: a plan and not quite enough time.
>
> —Leonard Bernstein

> Promise me you will not spend so much time treading water and trying to keep your head above the waves that you forget, truly forget, how much you have always loved to swim.
>
> —Tyler Knott Gregson

Scripture

God is our refuge and strength,
a very present help in trouble.
Therefore we will not fear, though the earth should change,
though the mountains shake in the heart of the sea;
though its waters roar and foam,
though the mountains tremble with its tumult. . . .
"Be still, and know that I am God!
I am exalted among the nations,
I am exalted in the earth."
The Lord of hosts is with us;
the God of Jacob is our refuge.
(Ps 46: 1–3, 10–11)

You're Not the Only One

> He said, "Go out and stand on the mountain before the Lord, for the Lord is about to pass by." Now there was a great wind, so strong that it was splitting mountains and breaking rocks in pieces before the Lord, but the Lord was not in the wind; and after the wind an earthquake, but the Lord was not in the earthquake; and after the earthquake a fire, but the Lord was not in the fire; and after the fire a sound of sheer silence. When Elijah heard it, he wrapped his face in his mantle and went out and stood at the entrance of the cave.
> (1 Kgs 19:11–13a)

I AM MOST DEFINITELY someone who has days where I feel completely overwhelmed by all that I have to do. It feels like there is no possible way that I can get it done. As a student, there tended to be three time periods each semester when I could almost guarantee this was going to happen, both in undergrad and grad school. The first would occur during the first couple days of the semester. I had not yet gotten back into the routine of the semester, so felt unsettled, and then when I got my syllabi I felt like I was already behind. And if I was already behind and it was only the first week, how could I ever catch up? The second would be around the middle of the term when midterms were at the heaviest, and again, the amount of work that I had to do—tests to study for, papers to get written, dreaded group projects to try and figure out—just didn't seem to be manageable. The third was about two weeks before classes ended. Finals loomed on the horizon along with everything else that had to be done for the end of classes. Those were the three times I could count on. Of course, there might also be other times. Maybe work or an extracurricular (marching band for me) was especially busy one week, cutting into homework time. I also found that as wonderful as it is to go spend a weekend at home, I never was able to get much work done, even when I knew I needed to. This could make going back to campus after a weekend home pretty stressful. Life happens, and that, combined with our workload, can leave us feeling overwhelmed.

When that happened, I'd typically call up one of my parents, near or already in tears, sometimes feeling almost paralyzed by the mountain of work that lay before me. Normally, the first thing my parents would say to me was, "Breathe." Nothing incredibly insightful and just one simple word, yet what an important word it is. Breathe. Get your breathing back to a normal pace and rhythm, let your heart calm down, let your body get the oxygen it needs. Take a deep breath. Breathe in, slowly let it out, repeat. Nothing is going to get done when you're freaking out (and while freaking out, I'd feel guilty about wasting time that I could be working instead of freaking out!). Once we got the breathing thing under control, they would ask me if I had made a to-do list (I love lists, so I often had one, but sometimes this had not yet happened). The list would give me a visual of everything that I needed to get done, allowing me to better prioritize and use my time wisely. I also take deep satisfaction from crossing something off my list. These are both part of why, even with all the technological ways I could make a to-do list, I most often still just write them down on paper because, for me, it allows better visualization and the satisfaction of physically crossing things off. I also learned when I get really stressed, it can be helpful to list the steps of a project. So instead of just "write paper," I might have something like: (1) outline paper; (2) write draft of paper; (3) create bibliography; (4) proof paper. Once the to-do list was created, the next piece of advice was to just start chipping away at it, one thing at a time.

When I get overwhelmed, some of the time it was just me freaking out and imagining myself to be in a far worse situation than I actually was in. This was typically true at the beginning of the semester, when I was adjusting back to what being a full-time student meant while figuring out what that semester was going to look like and when my good study times would be. Other times, my freaking out was over a legitimately worrisome amount of work to be done, more often than not resulting in part from my not getting stuff done ahead of time. In these instances, I sometimes needed to evaluate what needed to be done in comparison to the amount of time I had, as well as see if there was anything on my schedule that I could take off to free up some more time. I needed to look at what commitments I had made and where I had responsibilities, acknowledging I couldn't just not show up to something I had responsibilities for because I was stressed. This also helped me evaluate the extracurriculars I was involved with and if I really wanted to continue doing them. Sometimes the answer was no, and there were a few things I dropped over the course of my time at college. Other things I was a part of the entire time. One of the things that can be challenging to figure out in these stressful times is whether or not to let go of fun or social things on your calendar. Giving up the time to work can be hard, but sometimes what we need is some time spent with our friends to help us relax and see the bigger picture of life. Other times, we have to say no to some fun activities we would rather do than our work.

When I had more to do than I had time to get done, I also sometimes had to accept that things were not going to get done at the quality

I would like, and while that was hard, I would have to deal with it. It can help to develop an awareness of how much of the pressure is coming from the external sources, versus how much is internal pressure we are putting on ourselves. Sometimes it is mostly that, and it would be better to ask for an extension or for help than try to prove to ourselves we can handle it all. Likewise, for many of us it is helpful to have a routine. While it can be easy to get ourselves out of the routine when we get stressed, trying to maintain it as much as we can may allow us to remain more grounded as we work through everything.

Still, there will be times we feel underwater. In the midst of these overly stressful times, the times when you know your mind is likely to start racing uncontrollably in ways that are altogether unhelpful, it can be good to have ways to center yourself, allowing yourself to find calm or focus. Each of us will have our own ways that work for us, and the ones I share may not work for you. I invite you to try them though, as they have at some time worked for me. In one season, I used a phone app that guides you through five to ten minutes of stretching or yoga. I would go through this before I sat down to write, and it helped me clear my mind and allowed me to focus. It can help to get yourself out of your head and into a greater awareness of your body. This is also why there's the question my mom will ask in these moments—when did I last exercise? Normally, if I am in meltdown mode, it has been at least a week or two, which is not good for someone like me who even in college tried to exercise at least two to three times a week. My excuse was and is always that I haven't had time to spend exercising, and while my mom understands this, she also knows that exercising is a way to help my body blow off some steam and that part of what I am experiencing is actually a consequence of not exercising. Even just walking on a treadmill while reading articles for a class would help. For one student, knitting would help her get back into her body, and she could often do it while reading something. We need to care for our bodies in other ways too. Being exhausted also adds to making you feel overwhelmed, so even though you have way too much to get done, try to still get a decent night's sleep. Research tells us that all-nighters leave you worse off and your mind less sharp. It also helps to make sure you are trying to eat well, too, giving your body the nutrients it needs to support you.

During college and since, I have also learned several other ways to better ground and center myself, some of which use Ps 46:10a. At PCM, Pastor Ben taught us the two lines to a song. I later learned that there were more lines but repeating these two simple lines was perfect for me. The words were, "Peace be still and know that I am God," repeated twice. The music was written by a woman who went by Peace Pilgrim, and from 1953 through her death in 1981 walked over twenty-five thousand miles across the United States, vowing to "remain a wanderer until mankind has learned the way of peace, walking until given shelter and fasting until given food."[1] Whether it be a song like this or a Taize chant, it can be helpful to have a refrain you can use to center yourself and get you out of panic mode. You can also use this verse as a centering prayer. To do so, find a space where you can quiet your mind and body, be that in your room or by putting on headphones and some peaceful music wherever you are studying. At first, you can read the verse, but as you learn it, I invite you to close your eyes. After each line, allow at least five seconds to sit with what you just read. You may want to go through only the first five lines as you shorten the verse, or you may want to work back out to the full verse again.

> Be still and know that I am God
> Be still and know that I am
> Be still and know
> Be still
> Be
> Be still
> Be still and know
> Be still and know that I am
> Be still and know that I am God

Finally, something else that often helps me to re-center is to spend time out in nature, surrounding myself with the beauty of creation. For me, water is especially powerful, and I know it helps me to try to be by water on a regular basis. I don't get to the beach as much as I'd like to, but sitting and watching waves break is mesmerizing for me. I live between two rivers though, and the Schuylkill River Trail has in some years been voted the top urban trail in the country. So when I run or bike, I am able to go to water, and this helps. You may be at a school in a rural area where you can go for a walk and be in nature. Or you may be in a more urban area where you'll have to find green space, but do find a place to get away to when you need. Penn's campus has this pond randomly tucked on campus, which is a great little secluded spot and loved by many. When I'm in New York City, Bryant Park is my favorite little oasis, just a small park tucked amidst a bunch of

---

1. Friends of Peace Pilgrim, *Peace Pilgrim*, vi.

skyscrapers, and yet the perfect spot to be around trees and green. Growing up out west, it was a lot easier to see the night sky. Just walking to a dark area and looking up at the stars always made me feel overwhelmed at the vastness of the universe and reminded me that even though I was just a tiny little part of the universe, God still cares for me.

It seems that feeling overwhelmed has been an issue humanity has experienced possibly for as long as humans have been around, as is demonstrated to us by the words of Scripture. The psalmist felt overwhelmed, Elijah felt overwhelmed, and God was with both of them. People sometimes say things like "Let go and let God" or tell you to give it all to God, but in these instances, what does it mean to rely on God? While there are a lot of different beliefs about prayer and what prayer is and how it works, I'm not sure you'll find anyone who believes if you pray and ask God to do your homework for you, God will write your paper and you will find it there on your desktop just waiting for you to submit it. Letting go doesn't mean you get to not do anything, as much as we may want that to be the case. Still, as these Scriptures show us, it is important for God to be a part of the equation. We need to trust in God, but we have work to get done. Trusting in God can mean remembering that our value, our worth, is not tied up in these projects, that we have a much broader identity than only these assignments and even than our grades.

This passage about Elijah is a beautiful passage. One student pointed to it as a passage about taking care of our mental health, tending to our physical needs, and finding God in the quiet. What leads to this passage is Elijah feeling overwhelmed with the events that have happened, with his responsibility as a prophet of God, and with the fear that Jezebel is after his life. An angel shows up, offering him food and drink, and he journeys to Mt. Horeb and spends the night in the cave. When he wakes, God asks him what he is doing there. He says that he has been "zealous for the Lord" and for this they are trying to kill him. God tells him to stand at the mouth of the cave, where the Lord will pass by. We tend to expect that God is going to be present in big and powerful ways—Elijah looks for God in the wind and in the earthquake and in the fire, but it is in the sound of silence, or in some translations "sheer stillness," that Elijah finds God.

God is always present with us, helping to sustain us and give us strength, helping us to make it through the day. Sometimes, especially when we feel overwhelmed and panicked, we have to still ourselves to actually be able to remember this, to feel this. Elijah didn't find God in the noise or chaos; he found God when things were still. You may want to say that taking time to center yourself, to breathe or pray or take a quiet walk is a waste of time, that you could use those five to fifteen minutes to get more work done, but trust the wisdom of those who have gone before us (and the biology). What needs to get done will get done, one step at a time.

"Peace, be still, and know that I am God."

Prayer

Holy Spirit,
Calm the chaos within me,
The voices reminding me of all I have to get done,
The alarms going off telling me I am behind.
Let the tears help to wash away how completely overwhelmed I feel.
Allow me to rest in you entirely,
For just a few moments,
Long enough to find my center,
Long enough to feel your presence,
Long enough to quiet my racing heart,
And lengthen my too short breaths.
Remind me that I am only human,
And that no matter what I can or can't accomplish,
I am a beloved child of God,
Fearfully and wonderfully made.
Amen.

Reflection Questions

1. Do you tend to feel overwhelmed when you have a lot to get done? Are there patterns to the times when find yourself feeling overwhelmed? What are some of the things you might be able to do preemptively?

2. Do you have centering practices that you already use? Do you have a refrain that you can repeat to remind you that God is present? How might you incorporate this into each day?

3. Why do you think Elijah finds God in the stillness? What does this mean for our lives as disciples? What might this tell us about God?

4. What might the psalmist have been experiencing, personally or in their community, when they wrote these words found in Ps 46?

15

Perfectionism, Self-Expectations, and Being a Workaholic

How to Balance Work, Life, and Play

In fact, I would say that the demand for the perfect is the greatest enemy of true goodness. Perfection is a mathematical or divine concept; goodness is a beautiful human concept that includes every part of us and all of us.

—Richard Rohr

It is also hard to keep my expectations of myself
in check too at times, really hard.

—My Thesis Journal

Life is more fun if you play games.

—Roald Dahl

Scripture

Are you tired? Worn out? Burned out on religion? Come to me. Get away with me and you'll recover your life. I'll show you how to take a real rest. Walk with me and work with me—watch how I do it. Learn the unforced rhythms of grace. I won't lay anything heavy or ill-fitting on you. Keep company with me and you'll learn to live freely and lightly. (Matt 11:28–30 The Message)

You're Not the Only One

I'M ONE OF THOSE people who feel like there is never enough time in a day for everything I want to get done. I make a to-do list, guess how long it will take me, and all too often fill it up so that basically my whole day is accounted for. Then, the time I allowed to get something done turns out to be an underestimation of how long it actually will take, and all of a sudden, I thought I was going to get a lot more done than I actually do. You'd think I would learn, and try to adjust, and I sort of have. But I have very high expectations of myself and can get frustrated when I feel like something is taking more time than I want it too or isn't my best work. I say my temptation to border on being a workaholic is inherited—my grandfather, who died of pancreatic cancer, kept working half days as a lawyer until two days before he died. My mom inherited it from him, and I inherited it from her. At least that's one of the excuses I use. All of this can lead to feeling stressed and a sense of tension. I carry tension in my upper back and shoulders, which most of the time can end up being pretty tight, and some days it really can feel like I am carrying a burden (and a backpack filled with books can definitely feel like one too)!

As I mentioned in an earlier chapter, every semester I'd feel behind by the end of the first week. With all of my syllabi now in hand, I'd know what I was supposed to be doing and have a sense of what projects I should get started on and not wait until the last minute to do. There would be so much that I could read and write and work on that I'd decide I was already super behind and spend a couple of days really stressed out. Then I'd start chipping away at what all I needed to do. For most of undergrad, I'd error on the side of getting work done over taking a break to go play and have fun, a choice that at times was probably the best one for me, and at other times probably not. I initially had phrased that as being the "right one," which demonstrates how this continues to be an ongoing struggle for me. The reality is that this is not a matter of right and wrong, but is a reflection of our priorities, which can sometimes need adjusting as we try to find the right balance in our lives.

Fortunately, I had an experience studying abroad my junior year that helped to put my desire for perfection, along with my often unrealistic self-expectations, in perspective. Until I studied abroad, I had only ever experienced public schools in the United States, and that was the only grading system I was used to. I had always striven to get straight As, to the point of sacrificing other things for my grades at times. Typically, I had found that if I worked hard enough, I could get the A. At this point I had only gotten two

Perfectionism, Self-Expectations, and Being a Workaholic

Bs that I could remember—one in middle school band (I still contend that my teacher lost my practice sheet) and the other in a class I took the spring of my sophomore year of college (which I didn't study as much for because I assumed I knew the material—the "Epistles of Paul"—and had another class kicking my butt that I put a ton of time into and got an A). So in my head, working hard pretty much meant I could achieve the grades that only I expected of myself.

When I went to England, I discovered what I considered to be some of the idiosyncrasies of the British grading system. This included that at the University of East Anglia, where I studied, it was pretty much impossible to get a "first" on a paper in a liberal arts class. The British grading system is completely different than ours, which is probably why my grades were transferring back as pass/fail. When I say that their grading system is completely different—it is. If you get between a 70 and 100 percent on something, that is a first, or the highest grade you can get. On one of my first papers, I got a 68 percent, a grade my flatmates told me was an excellent grade. Well, that in and of itself was weird, a 68 percent is really good? It was hard to break out of the notion that this was a D! The other thing I was told is that they don't give above 70 percent pretty much ever, so try as I might, it looked like the best grade I could get was a 2:1 (the second highest). Getting what would be considered top marks (or the highest grade) was out of my control. I still worked hard, but this forced me to accept that I could not always get the grades I desired. It helped me to let go, at least a little, of my obsession with grades and to focus on learning what I could and enjoying my time abroad, realizing time in the kitchen with flatmates may have been more valuable than what I learned in the classroom. It also helped, to some extent, with my being less obsessed with my grades when I returned, and more willing to take classes pass/fail, especially in grad school. I can't say I didn't still focus on grades, or that I wasn't often driven by them, but studying abroad created a freedom for me I had not experienced before. It reminded me that the primary value of our education and my own worth as a student isn't measured solely by the grade we receive.

I have never been able to fully understand where my self-expectations come from. My parents wanted us to do our best, which meant putting in effort, but they didn't demand we achieve a certain GPA or anything like that. School is what I was good at, which I think is part of what made me want to do so well. I was not a good athlete, I wasn't especially attractive, I was definitely not the class clown, but I was smart, and teachers noticed and affirmed my work in classes. I was a bookworm who got scolded in multiple classes for reading when I was supposed to be doing other things (my sixth-grade teacher called me "pony girl" because I always had a book about horses with me that I would read whenever I could—*The Saddle Club*, *Thoroughbred*, Marguerite Henry books—if it was about horses, I was in). I poured myself into learning, and I enjoyed it.

Loving learning and having a tendency towards perfectionism are definitely not the same thing though. I love learning, and I have always expected a great deal of myself. I still get frustrated with myself at times when I don't feel I have accomplished the amount or quality of work that I think I should have been able to get done. When I start to wonder "What will others think of me?" I often have to check myself and realize that these are expectations I have put onto myself, and that the "other people" whose perception I'm worried about don't actually have the same expectations of me. Our culture and society don't help us either. We live in a culture that prizes production and achievement, that can make us feel like even our leisure activities need to have something tangible that results from them. This can add to the expectations we have for ourselves if we are always trying to live up to what we think the world demands of us instead of what is best for us, what God wants for us.

So often we create the burdens that we carry; we opt to shoulder responsibilities that God hasn't asked us to. In this passage, Jesus offers us an alternative, a way to live differently. Sometimes, we need a total change in lifestyle to see what this could mean, in my case literally going to another country (again) and another place. Jesus invites us to "Learn the unforced rhythms of grace." For the longest time, I'm not sure I could have told you what this meant, until I felt like I experienced it. To experience it, I had to leave the patterns of my normal life in a culture obsessed with productivity and travel to a fairly remote location on the northern coast of Northern Ireland, where I didn't have an international plan so my phone only worked when I had Wi-Fi. During one of my summers in seminary, I spent almost a month volunteering at Corrymeela, a Christian community focused on peace and reconciliation. As a volunteer, you help keep things functioning. You have four-day rotations and do everything from working in the kitchen to housekeeping to helping assist the groups that are staying at Corrymeela, some of whom have the Corrymeela staff facilitate their time at this incredible place. Unlike on a relaxing vacation, as a volunteer you are working and there is a good amount to be done.

Perfectionism, Self-Expectations, and Being a Workaholic

During my time there, I just felt like I was living in a way that seemed like how we were created to live. It may sound weird, but I felt more in tune with the natural rhythms of the earth while I was there. This felt more like how God created us to live, in rhythms that have gotten thrown off by the schedules we try to keep and by how disconnected we often are from nature. Being on a cliff overlooking the sea, where the water rhythmically met the land, may have been a part of this, but this is also just a wonderfully sacred place, a thin place. Everything seemed in balance: work, rest, worship, play, community. I wasn't stressed, but I was still being a productive human being. When I then read the version of this passage from The Message, this phrase jumped out to me: "the unforced rhythms of grace." Maybe Jesus was showing me a better way in my time at Corrymeela, a way that I would have to be intentional to create once I got back home.

At Corrymeela, there also was a very natural blending of faith and work. Too often, the long list we have of things to get done and our life of faith have absolutely nothing to do with each other. How do we work to shape our lives in such a way that we are living every moment for God, through God, in God? How can you devote your studies, your job, your time spent with friends to God? When we are able to do this, does it help us shift our expectations away from performance to being a part of a bigger picture and story? Does it allow us to take Jesus up on his offer to take our yoke and replace it with one that is light and easy to bear?

In all of this, there is also a need for joy, and often for play, though we may be figuring out what play looks like for us as we grow up. At Corrymeela, I would play with children from the groups visiting the space, but I also found space for play with the other volunteers. When I was in senior high, one of the things I remember my mom doing with the youth group was having events and sometimes even retreats around the theme of being a child of God. The point wasn't just that we all belong to God or that God is our heavenly parent, there was an emphasis on being a kid, on remembering our inner child. We are so often in such a hurry to grow up, as teenagers and then as college students. As teenagers, we no longer want to be considered a child; we want the rights and privileges that come with being seen as old enough and responsible enough to make our own choices. As a college student, we're in a liminal space—given many of the perks of being an adult, as well as some of the challenges, but for many of us, we also feel that we are not quite there yet. During these phases of life, we can seek to push away that which we consider childish, too young, or not adult enough.

You're Not the Only One

There is so much of the play of childhood that we need, though. The creativity, laughter, wonder, and just fun that releasing our inner child can foster is healthy and necessary, but we sometimes need permission for it to feel okay. That is why my mom would create events for high schoolers where we would do things that reminded us of our childhoods, and why I continued the tradition as I went into college and beyond. Both at PCM when I was an undergrad and at the CA as a campus minister, I've created events to celebrate being children of God. At PCM, we put our hair in pigtails, ate chicken nuggets, and played Hungry Hungry Hippos. My senior year, Cassie and I hosted a Disney party, where we dressed up like Disney characters and watched old Disney movies from when we were younger. One of the CA's senior send-off celebrations for our graduates was a throwback to their elementary school days, complete with Gushers, childhood pictures, and chalk and bubbles to play with outside. It can be easy to feel silly in these moments and even to feel ashamed or embarrassed if seen by others, but it's good to be a kid every now and then. In a world that seems to ask adults and sometimes even adolescents to carry many burdens, moments of childhood fun can be a time to set those burdens down and embrace who God created us to be.

We live in a culture that promotes productivity and independence, often at the expense of our well-being. We carry our own expectations of ourselves and our performance that can be hard to let go. At the same time, we worship a God who Scripture tells us claims us as children and offers to take the heavy burdens we are carrying and give us one that is light and easy instead. Are we willing to seek out the ways in which we can set down, at least for a time, the heavy burdens of life and our self-expectations that we carry, embrace the beauty of play, and learn the unforced rhythms of grace? Can we seek a better balance in the lives that God has given us?

Prayer

Jesus,
You walk this journey with us,
And offer to carry our yoke.
You show us how to live a life where we
Don't have to carry the heavy weight of expectations,
Those we have created for ourselves or from others.
Help us learn to live as your children,
Created to contribute to this world,

Perfectionism, Self-Expectations, and Being a Workaholic

But also created for balance,
To live in tune with the rhythms of the planet.
Allow us to let go of our unrealistic expectations of ourselves,
And to address expectations placed on us by others.
Allow us to not let perfection become the enemy of goodness,
But to seek goodness.
Remind us to find childlike wonder and joy,
To allow space for play in our lives.
Thank you for teaching us how you would have us live.
Amen.

REFLECTION QUESTIONS

1. What kind of expectations do you feel are placed on you? Where do they come from? Do you have a lot of self-expectations?

2. Do you incorporate play into your life? If so, how? What are some of your favorite memories from being a kid, and how can those experiences transfer to today? If your childhood didn't allow you to be a child, how might you want to find ways to incorporate play into your life now?

3. What does "Learn the unforced rhythms of grace" mean to you? How can we strive to live this way? What does it mean to recover your life?

16

Mind, Body, Soul

Tending to Your Well-Being

Through the Sabbath, God tells us another story. It's a story that doesn't do away with our work. It's a story that puts our work in perspective. It's a story of rest and grace. . . . Grace messes with us, especially if we're hard-working types from anywhere who know how to get stuff done. Grace disorients us. But grace also provides us with an extraordinary promise. Before we existed, before we could do anything to earn it, we were loved.

—Nate Stucky

Wisdom is not gained by knowing what is right. Wisdom is gained by practicing what is right, and noticing what happens when that practice succeeds and when it fails.

—Barbara Brown Taylor

Scripture

Have you not known? Have you not heard?
The Lord is the everlasting God
the Creator of the ends of the earth.
He does not faint or grow weary;
his understanding is unsearchable.
He gives power to the faint,
and strengthens the powerless.
Even youths will faint and be weary,

and the young will fall exhausted;
but those who wait for the Lord shall renew their strength,
they shall mount up with wings like eagles,
they shall run and not be weary,
they shall walk and not faint.
(Isa 40:28–31)

WITH EVERYTHING THAT IS going on in college, it can be hard to set aside time to take care of yourself. In order to stay healthy, feeling good, and even to get the most you can out of college, it is vital to take care of you. This doesn't mean just physically either. It means considering our lives holistically and developing ways to tend to this wonderful life that God has given us, to nurture our body, mind, and soul. Each of these parts of ourselves needs to be exercised and needs time for rest as well. Taking time now to form good habits can provide you with practices you can carry with you for the rest of your life.

Life is a beautiful mix of things that feel sacred and things that feel secular, or maybe just ordinary, but the reality is that it is all intertwined, and that everything is sacred. This is true when it comes to your body as well, and your body was created to give you feedback on how you are doing at taking care of yourself. Learning to listen to your body—when it needs rest, when it needs activity, when it is stressed, etc.—can be a critical part of learning how to take care of yourself. It provides us with warning signs that something may not be quite right in our lives. When we are too busy, it can be easy to miss or ignore those signs, which is one of the reasons why Sabbath and rest are so important.

Let's look at these three dimensions that we often break life into—our mind, our body, and our soul—and what it means to care for each one, while also recognizing that they are all so intricately intertwined that taking care of and listening to each also takes care of the other parts of us. When it comes to exercising the mind, you won't have to go far at college. This is a time of life where there are a plethora of opportunities to expand your mind, and with all the work you will be doing for classes, it's unlikely that your brain is going unused, as long as you choose to apply it. You will have more say now in the ways your mind will be stretched than you have had in school before, so this is a time to take advantage of the opportunities to learn and grow. Take electives that will actually be interesting for you, things that might allow you to learn about facets of life that you won't study in your major. It's possible that there will be a guest lecturer or panel on your campus almost every night that you could attend, so pick out a couple each month and go. Learn to do new things, join a club or intramural team, or find a class somewhere nearby in the community. I spent a semester taking a tennis course at a nearby community college, and while I still could barely play at the end of the semester in any kind of sustained fashion, it was something I was glad I tried out.

This can be a great time to learn some new life skills. Depending on how much you cooked before you went to college, some of these skills might be in the kitchen. I have seen people learn a lot in the kitchen, both when I was in college and in my work at the CA. From how to use a can opener to what oven mitts are, to how to make scrambled eggs and pancakes, to how to take soup that's been frozen and make it hot and edible, the CA kitchen is a place not only of fellowship but of learning. This all feeds your mind and often helps feed your body as well. There are lots of other life skills you could seek out. I've helped to teach students how to sew, budget, and build a garden bed before. You could learn a new language or learn how to code. College is full of ways to feed your mind.

Our brains also need time to rest. Sleep is important, but only one part of this. We also need practices to help quiet our minds, such as centering prayer or meditation. I also find that some forms of exercise help do this for me, especially ones that require me to focus on what I am doing. Swimming laps where I can focus on my breathing, or rock climbing where I have to focus on staying on the wall, are forms of exercise that also take my mind off of other things. Swimming laps is also a place where I will often spend time talking to God, and while it is time in prayer, it is very casual and chatty in nature, and I often think about God talking back to me with a little bit of sass. When your brain needs a break, taking a few minutes just to stretch can be a good place to start. Creative forms of expression, such as painting or coloring, are another good way for many people to help quiet their minds. If I find myself being especially forgetful or I feel like I could just fall asleep, I know that my mind is probably not getting the rest that it needs to function its best and that attending to it with a good night's sleep will make tomorrow a much better day.

Obviously, as we see throughout this chapter, our mind, body, and soul are intermingled, as are the ways we nurture each. The impacts of not just our phones but also social media on each part of our lives are real too. They have positive aspects. They connect us to friends and family, sometimes are the source for some of the new things we might be learning through an app, and can also provide creative outlets. We also know that our phones can have negative impacts on our lives, from feeling like we always are available, to comparing our lives to the curated lives others portray on their social media, to algorithms that are meant to get us agitated. Sometimes our brains need a break from our phones, even from the positive things they provide us. Sometimes we just need to let our brains shut off for a bit.

As we shift from focusing on the mind to focusing on taking care of your body, it again includes sleep, as well as exercise and also what you eat. My diet was often one of the ways I could measure how well I was taking care of myself. Typically, around the beginning of finals week, I would make a batch of Funfetti cupcakes, which I liked better unfrosted. Those cupcakes and cereal were pretty much the bulk of what I lived off of during finals week, with maybe a couple of peanut butter and jelly sandwiches thrown in too. It wasn't the best of diets. When I was taking better care of myself, that was also reflected in how I ate, which would then tend to be more balanced and include things from all of the different food groups (okay, maybe I was never great about eating veggies). Students have also commented on the challenges of making the right choices when you have a meal swipe system and can pick whatever you want each night. One mentioned that eating cheeseburgers every night ends up not being the best way to take care of your body.

I may not be the best person to talk to about sleep. As I mention elsewhere, I didn't really get enough during college. After I graduated and began grad school, my body decided it could no longer function off the amount of sleep I had been getting and started demanding I get at least seven hours of sleep most nights to function. If I were to choose not to listen to what my body was telling me, I would feel it, either in exhaustion or getting sick. Over time, I have found that my sweet spot is right around seven to seven-and-a-half hours of sleep each night, and now, my body often wakes up before my alarm. I have friends who need closer to nine hours of sleep. Every body is different, and you should figure out what works best for you. Also, the environment in which you sleep really does matter, as does how you go to bed. Falling asleep while studying is not going to give you a great night's sleep, and you probably know that in the ideal world it's best to have some time without screens before you fall asleep (i.e., don't get into bed and stare at your phone for an hour). Try to create an environment conducive to sleep for yourself. Most importantly, listen to your body! One thing I learned is that I tended to push hard all semester, and then get home for break and end up with a bad cold or other nasty virus. I ended up treating the symptom instead of the cause, just planning to take it easy my first few days after the semester ended in case I got sick. Had I done a better job trying to get more rest regularly during the semester, I might have been able to avoid these unpleasant illnesses altogether.

I've also learned that exercise has a huge role to play in my physical and mental well-being. As I've mentioned before, sometimes when I'm feeling out of sorts, my mom will ask me when I last exercised. While the question is often irritating, I'd guess that at least 80 percent of the time she asks the question, I won't have been getting enough exercise, which impacts my mood. Getting exercise at college can be achieved fairly easily if you put in a little effort, and often in some fun ways. Depending on the geography of your campus, walking to and from classes keeps many students fairly active. Sometimes the activities you are involved in will also be how you get exercise, as marching band did for me. With at least ten hours on the field most weeks, I definitely was kept in shape. During the spring semester, when I did not have marching band rehearsal, I had to put in more effort to get myself to exercise. I would try to go swim regularly, as this was before I started running. Sometimes I had more success than others. During my final semester of college, I tried something new as well. Erin, Shad, Mike, and I all got memberships to the local rock gym and would go two or three times every week. Going with friends was a lot of fun, and because you needed at least two to belay one another, we helped get each other to go to the gym. It was a great work out and helped to tone my muscles. Plus, it was a mental workout as you figured out the path you were going to take up the wall. Even with exercise, your body needs rest, and it's important to not overwork your body, to listen to your muscles when they want a day off.

Last, but definitely not least, it is important that we take care of our soul. Exercising our soul means engaging in spiritual practices and relationships that help us continue to grow in our faith, that can lead to new ways of encountering the triune God. Let's be real—getting to church on Sunday mornings can be hard during college. If you can find a church community that fits, it can be worth it though. It's also worth exploring other opportunities as well. When I went to PCM, we had worship on Tuesday nights, and at the CA we've had it on Wednesday nights. Some of the students still go to church on Sundays, and others say that the mid-week worship is their "Sunday morning." College was also a time I found some great books about

Mind, Body, Soul

faith and living as a Christian that both helped me articulate a lot of my own thoughts and beliefs and also provided for conversations with friends who read the same books.

Rest for the soul can mean rest for our whole selves. While I was in seminary, I met Nate, who was working on his PhD. One of the things Nate cares about is helping others understand what it means that on the seventh day of creation, God rested, and that we, too, were created in such a way that our lives need a rhythm that involves rest and resting in God. This doesn't mean sitting in church for the entirety of Sunday. It does mean breaking your pattern, and creating a space that is intentionally different, that allows for you to focus on connecting with God above all else.

I remember a class Nate led talking about Sabbath and how keeping Sabbath actually allows us to live more fully into who we want to be and who we are called to be. Our class full of seminary students had lots of excuses for why it was really hard to keep some type of Sabbath, but we were told this was no excuse for not finding time for Sabbath. Nate's lesson involved rubber duckies and *Sesame Street*. In a Sesame Street sketch that some of you might remember, Ernie has a problem and goes to Hoots the Owl for help.[1] Ernie is trying to learn how to play the saxophone but has a rubber duck he won't let go of. Every time he tries to play the saxophone, the duck squeaks and ruins his playing. Hoots tells him he sees what his problem is and tells Ernie he has to put the duckie down to allow him to play the saxophone. Eventually, after being encouraged by many people, Ernie does and plays the saxophone quite well. He also finds out he can pick his duck back up after he has finished. Nate used this illustration to talk about how the rubber duckies in our lives are the things we would argue we couldn't put down in order to take a Sabbath: homework, chores, things we had to get done, etc. In order to live in the way God created us to live, we have to put down our duckies, at least for a while.

Sabbath means setting aside time to spend with God, to do things that replenish your soul, and bring you into communion with your creator. Play might be a part of your Sabbath! Gathering with friends for a meal or to play board games can be Sabbath, as can taking a hike or just finding a peaceful spot in nature to sit and take in your surroundings. Also, Sabbath doesn't have to be something you jump into as a whole twenty-four hours

---

1. If you search "Put Down the Duckie" online, you can find videos of the original or one of the several reprisals that have been done on *Sesame Street*. For example, see Sesame Street, "Ernie Learns."

or nothing at all. Set aside what time you can, and if it is not very much right now, set a goal to grow it, little by little, until you have created a pattern where you have more.

College is a time in which there can be lots of duckies. In addition to the things just mentioned, there are extracurriculars, jobs, group projects, study groups, and often the sense that you have more to do than you have time to get done. In a context like this, what does it mean to talk about taking care of yourself and doing so in a way that equally takes care of your mind, body, and soul? The passage from Isaiah reminds us that even youth like you grow tired and weary. It tells us to "wait" for the Lord or wait upon the Lord, or in some other translations, to hope in the Lord or trust in the Lord (lots of small differences in translation!). Waiting might mean resting, waiting to get on with that long to-do list you have. Hoping and trusting might mean believing that God knows what is best for us and gave us bodies that communicate what they need to us when we take the time to listen. God is our strength, and God has given us the tools to strengthen ourselves too. God knows we need to take care of ourselves—all of ourselves, our intertwined mind, body, and soul—if we are to flourish in the way God intended for us.

Prayer

Triune God,
You created the world,
And then you rested.
You created us in your image,
Needing both work and rest.
Yet our world and our lives seem so busy.
It can be hard to slow down,
And we can ignore the needs of our minds, bodies, and souls.
Help us to take care of ourselves,
To create opportunities to grow and to rest.
Teach us what it means to have Sabbath in our lives,
And how to put down the duckie so we might do so.
Help us live lives where we not only respect the life you have given us,
But where we use that life to live into all you created us to be
When we wait for the Lord.
Amen.

Mind, Body, Soul

Reflection Questions

1. Do you listen to your body? What are some examples you have of when your body has tried to tell you that you are off balance before? What are some examples of times where you have been in balance?

2. How do you exercise your mind, your body, and your soul? How do you provide rest for each?

3. What does Sabbath mean or look like to you? What are some things that you might do during Sabbath time? How would these practices help you connect with God and re-center yourself? What activities do you think are less compatible with Sabbath?

17

Owning Your Own Paradox

Contradictions are not impediments to the spiritual life; rather, they are an integral part of the spiritual life. Every highly conscious person I have met has struggled with more than one deep contradiction. Contradictions don't encourage you to abandon your critical faculties, but to sharpen them. . . . The reconciling third isn't necessarily a third opinion. It's much more subtle than that. The third way acknowledges: "That is true and that is true, too, and I've got to learn to coexist with both of them." It's not fully a third position, but a holding tank where you recognize the truth that's in both positions without trying to dismiss either one of them. That's not easy. I believe it's uniquely the work of the Spirit to help you "build the house of wisdom" (Proverbs 9:1) and to hold the tension.

—RICHARD ROHR

The goofy thing about Christian faith is that you believe it and you don't believe it at the same time.

—DONALD MILLER

Inconsistencies, imperfections, and failures to live up to ideals are all part of what it means to be human. What seems to distinguish those who are most deeply and wholly human is not their perfection, but their courage in accepting their imperfections. Accepting themselves as they are, they then become able to accept others as they are.

—DAVID BENNER

Owning Your Own Paradox

SCRIPTURE

> He said, "Go out and stand on the mountain before the Lord, for the Lord is about to pass by." Now there was a great wind, so strong that it was splitting mountains and breaking rocks in pieces before the Lord, but the Lord was not in the wind; and after the wind an earthquake, but the Lord was not in the earthquake; and after the earthquake a fire, but the Lord was not in the fire; and after the fire a sound of sheer silence. When Elijah heard it, he wrapped his face in his mantle and went out and stood at the entrance of the cave. (1 Kgs 19:11–13a)

HAVING FELT CALLED TO ministry since eighth grade, I had known what I planned to do with my life for a long time before I finally got to my senior year of college. Earlier in college, I had thought about taking a year off before grad school to do a volunteer year. By my senior year, I realized I was looking forward to seminary too much and would spend the year just waiting to start grad school. Then I became a hot mess, largely because I felt like my faith and my call were a living paradox, one that I couldn't imagine would make me a good pastor. I was in the process of applying to seminary, and I still felt called to be a minister. At the same time, I was struggling deeply. I had so, so many questions and doubts. I thought pastors are supposed to be the ones you go to when you have questions because they have answers and wisdom. I couldn't believe that anyone would really want someone who had all these questions and doubts, someone with all these uncertainties, someone like me, to be their pastor. I was sitting in Dr. Swaim's office crying one day, telling her all of this. I remember, probably almost verbatim, her response to me. She told me that she had absolutely no doubt that I was called to be a pastor and to go and be a minister for those who had questions and doubts just like I did. Little did I know how prophetic her comment would be. Indeed, I would go on to be a pastor for those very much like myself in that moment, college students who have lots of questions and doubts, as well as adults of all ages who have them too. Now I know many pastors, whether they will openly say so or not, also have questions and doubts, and that they are a healthy part of our lives of faith. Some days, though, I still feel the tension between my questions, doubts, and my Christian identity.

You're Not the Only One

Paradoxes are interesting because we often perceive them to be contradictory when there is actually space for both pieces. We can't quite figure out what is going on, who or what we are supposed to be. The answer may be that it's a complex mix of all of the above. During this stage of life, the time many young people spend at college, you are largely in a stage of transition. There are so many ways we can feel as if parts of ourselves just don't quite align. This often feels incredibly uncomfortable, but most of the time, the answer doesn't have to be just one or the other. I don't have to be a kid or an adult, feminine or a tomboy, an intellectual or someone who likes to have fun, the person my family and friends knew back home or the person I am becoming at school, a pastor or someone who sometimes doubts faith all together. I can be all of these things. The challenge is to learn to embrace the paradox, and learn how to be a coherent being who also has your own quirks and inconsistencies, some of which may be permanent and some pieces of ourselves that are in progress.

During your college years, age, or more so your stage of life, can feel hard to understand; it can be hard to figure out quite what you are. I know when I talk about music I date myself, but one of the songs that came out when I was in high school was Britney Spears's "I'm Not a Girl, Not Yet a Woman." In college, I found myself resonating with the sentiment of the song, and also deeply disturbed that a Britney Spears song was expressing my emotional struggle of growing up. If I am honest, there were times I wanted to be seen as an adult, times I just wanted to be a kid, and times where I wished it was possible to be both. These four or so years, and sometimes even a few years after them, feel like this weird in-between phase, where you don't really feel ready for "adulthood" (in some ways I'm not sure you ever do), yet you are now more independent than you were as a kid. Legally speaking, you are an adult. When you are at school or work, when you're away from your childhood home, you are largely responsible for taking care of you. You have to figure out food, do your laundry, get yourself to the doctor when you get sick, etc. At the same time, when you go home, you may find that you are not treated as an adult, and this can be confusing and challenging. You feel perceived as being a kid and it's frustrating. Then there are the times you really just want to be a kid. You want to play, to have child-like fun, maybe have a parent do the laundry you brought home, but sometimes wonder if this makes you less of an adult (it doesn't, maybe minus the laundry part!). Indeed, this is a time when in many ways you are living in the in-between, a liminal space.

Owning Your Own Paradox

At a time when, both consciously and unconsciously, you are focused on identity development, there will be a lot of pieces of your identity that may not feel like they fit together, and yet both are truly part of you. Some struggle with being a person of faith and a scientist, only to find the more they learn about science the more they feel they learn about God. You may feel like if you have one identity—an athlete, sorority, fraternity, marching band or orchestra member, part of this club or that—then people won't also let you have some other identity. The reality is that we are all complex individuals, and growing in who we are means embracing all of who we are. Owning your paradoxes is also about learning who you are and how to be comfortable in your own skin. We are often gentler with others as they figure this out for themselves, but this is also something we need to remember both with our friends and with others. We are all works in progress, and we all deserve to be given space to figure ourselves out (at least as long as we are not hurting others in the process).

Part of this conversation sometimes involves figuring out pieces of our identity that do not fit the stereotypes society may place on those identities. One of my own internal paradoxes has always been around gender. When I was in college, there was very little discussion around non-binary identities. I am very grateful for students today that there is a broader spectrum of ways for people to identify themselves and explore who they are and the identity that fits them best. This is also a cross-generational conversation, and society has looked different as each generation has come of age. However you choose to identify, you may find that you feel like you don't fit the stereotypical mold in every way, as has often been the case with my identifying as a woman.

I have often wondered what it means to own my own womanhood, even my femininity, without letting it solely define me or what I am capable of. On good days, I remember that I get to help define what these things might mean and look like. Other days, the stereotypes from other parts of Christianity, and from Western society at large, can feel exhausting to fight against. Over the years, as I continue to figure out how to best express who I am, this has presented in different ways. This has been the case since I was a child. I was never a girly-girl. I think somewhere in my mind being girly and being smart, or being self-sufficient and independent, seemed at odds. One consequence of this was that until about the age of twelve, I refused to wear pink. I'm sure I had some things that had pink in a pattern, and I did have this dress I wore pretty much every time we played dress-up for years

You're Not the Only One

that was this awful pink/purple/brown/dirty-from-too-much-wear color, but if we went shopping and there was a pink top, no way was I about to try it on. Pink was girly, and I was not about to have any of that, especially when it came to fashion. Late elementary school was probably the worst, when the popular girls at school were starting to be really into fashion and boys. Around middle school, I allowed a few pink things to enter my wardrobe, but not much. I did have a few friends who were similar to me in this way, but it also felt like we were "odd" in the eyes of some of our peers. Although this sometimes felt painful and lonely, school and intelligence were far more important to me than looks. At the same time, while not wanting to wear "girly" clothing, when I chose an instrument to play in band in fourth grade, I decided to play the flute. In eighth grade, when I picked a language to study, I chose French because it seemed romantic (despite the fact that I lived four hours from the Mexican border and in a state with a large Spanish-speaking population). We all are ultimately living paradoxes. Part of me wants to embrace the feminine in me, in sometimes stereotypic ways, and part of me wants to push back on the gender norms that our society sometimes seems to force on us. It's possible to do both, even if that means not living with a perfectly consistent or coherent way of being.

My sister called me one day after getting out of class while studying for her master's in social work, to tell me we were less typical then even we realized. She and I loved playing with K'nex growing up. We built the Big Ball Factory, we built a roller coaster, we spent weeks putting together these structures by connecting the little pieces to make something bigger. When her class talked about toys and gender that day, she was the only female in the room to have played with K'nex as a kid, and she still has them today! I grew up learning skills that have given me a wide variety of abilities and make me feel empowered, and while some may want to categorize them as one thing or another, they are all just part of me. I learned to bake, something I still love doing, and to sew, which I started doing a lot more of during and since the COVID-19 pandemic. When my dad started traveling more for work, he taught me how to take care of the technology issues in the house while he was gone. In high school, when I started going on service trips, I learned construction skills—how to use a hammer, a circular saw, do some basic electrical wiring, and more—and loved it. At the same time, I'm not sure I could change a diaper, then or now. We are all capable of learning all kinds of skills, of doing many things, and we shouldn't let what society tells us we should or shouldn't do based on our identities stop us from pursuing the things that interest us.

This can play out in a number of ways for each of us. Our gender identities are just one of the ways that society will create boxes they expect us to fit in, but so will a number of our other identities, including our faith tradition. Most likely, we won't always fit in them, nor should we. While sometimes people will make you feel like a paradox in the various ways you choose to live into who you are, the beautiful thing is that you are just who God has created you to be, so lean into it.

We should acknowledge, however, that we do have inconsistencies that should be attended to. Sometimes they indicate behaviors that we may need to address, like if we find ourselves lying or cheating or making other choices that do not feel consistent with the person we want to be. Other times, they may be things we should think about and be aware of even if they cannot be resolved. For instance, if my faith calls me to think about how the least of these are treated, what does that mean about the things I buy such as food, clothes, and technology? Do I think about the impact of my purchases and my actions on other people or on the planet? Many of these are in part the results of societal structures of sin, which are incredibly hard to dismantle, and it's easy to quickly feel overwhelmed. These inconsistencies cannot often be easily resolved, but they are important to be aware of and to keep growing in. Likewise, if I call myself Christian, does how I treat others in my everyday encounters bear witness to that identity?

To me, part of exploring our personal paradoxes is about taking a moment to explore the areas of our lives that make us go "huh," that leave us a bit surprised by what we didn't really expect to see. This Scripture passage about Elijah from 1 Kings tells of Elijah finding God where he least expected to (and yes, I'm aware the same Scripture showed up a few chapters back. I like it.). Elijah, like a number of other figures in the Bible, had gotten himself into a rough patch, and instead of relying upon God, decided to have a pity party for himself (also like a number of other people in the Bible). Queen Jezebel had commanded her prophets to challenge Elijah to see which of them worshiped the true God, and Elijah had won. Elijah then killed Jezebel's prophets, so now she is trying to kill Elijah. He flees. God leads him to Mt. Horeb, and there Elijah spends the night in a cave. Then God tells him to go to the mouth of the cave, for the Lord is about to pass by. When we think about God, when we think about wanting a reminder of how mighty and awesome God is, we want strong shows of force and power, right? That's probably what Elijah was expecting, yet God wasn't in the mighty wind, or the earthquake, or the fire. God was in "the sound of sheer silence," a phrase which is itself a paradox! This is one of those Hebrew words that is fun because it gets translated in these nuanced ways, sometimes it's a whisper, calm, stillness; one translation even says a "gentle blowing" (NASB). The word only shows up two other places—in Ps 107, where it's used to talk about God stilling the waves, and in Job 4, where it is used similarly to how it is used here—hearing stillness and a voice. What we should take away from all of this is that God shows up where it's least expected. God is all powerful yet speaks in the gentlest of whispers. Maybe, as we are created in God's image, there is some divinity in what seems like our personal paradoxes. Our lives are meant to be beautiful, creative mosaics (or K'nex masterpieces), with all colors and types of glass pieces coming together to make the whole, a picture that takes a lifetime to create.

PRAYER

Creative God,
You constantly show up in the places and ways
We least expect you to,
Surprising us,
Reminding us of your power and might,
Captured in the gentlest of whispers.
Allow us to be surprised by ourselves,
By the power inside each of us,
By the beautiful mosaic of quirky interests,
Strengths, gifts and passions,
That you have given each of us.
Help us to embrace who we are,
To soften the sharp edges,
And to respond with grace to ourselves
And to others.
Amen.

Owning Your Own Paradox

REFLECTION QUESTIONS

1. Describe some of the pieces you see comprising the mosaic that is you. What color and texture of glass might you choose to represent some of the parts of your identity?

2. Where do you feel the tension of paradoxes in your own identity? Are these pieces really at odds with one another, or just different components of who you are?

3. Are there some paradoxes or inconsistencies in who we are that might not be good, and that we should work to change? What might these be? How might God help?

18

Studying Abroad

When I Was the One with the Accent

Travel, for me, is a little bit like being in love, because suddenly all your senses are at the setting marked "on." Suddenly you're alert to the secret patterns of the world. The real voyage of discovery, as Marcel Proust famously said, consists not in seeing new sights, but in looking with new eyes. And of course, once you have new eyes, even the old sights, even your home becomes something different.

—Pico Iyer

Not till we are lost, in other words not till we have lost the world, do we begin to find ourselves, and realize where we are and the infinite extent of our relations.

—Henry David Thoreau

Scripture

When an alien resides with you in your land, you shall not oppress the alien. The alien who resides with you shall be to you as the citizen among you; you shall love the alien as yourself, for you were aliens in the land of Egypt: I am the Lord your God. (Lev 19:33–34)

Studying Abroad

WHEN I CHOSE TO attend an in-state college, one of the requirements my parents set was that I spend a semester abroad. They wanted me to experience not being close to home and what it is like to live someplace different, as Phoenix and Tucson are pretty similar in many ways. So, on my twenty-first birthday, after going out to lunch with my family so I could legally order a drink, I flew across the Atlantic Ocean. I was headed to the University of East Anglia (UEA), in Norwich, England, where the drinking age was eighteen and nobody cared that I was now twenty-one. Already nervous about traveling thousands of miles on my own to spend the next five months in a strange place, things started off a bit rocky. When I arrived, I had been traveling for hours and was tired and hungry (and this was long before Uber or Lyft existed; it was even before smart phones). I went to the office to check in, where they discovered that there had been a mistake with the room assignments and I didn't have a dorm room assigned for me. There also was only one place on campus I could get food after 8:00 p.m., which is when I had arrived. There was, however, a room being repaired that would be available within a couple of days, so after eating at the only place still open and spending a night in a spare room, I moved into my home for the next five months.

The mistake ended up being a wonderful thing! It meant I got to be in a flat with all British flatmates, which not a lot of the international students got to do (most were housed with other international students). I was in the new flats that had recently been built about a ten-minute walk from campus. My flat had seven other students besides myself in it. We each had our own bowling alley room with a very small shower/bathroom pod, and then shared a kitchen and eating area. As only first years get to live on campus, most of my flatmates were eighteen and in their first year of university, though there were two females who were doing medical programs who were older than me. There were six of us—these two females and three of the males—who spent a lot of time together, sitting in the hall talking, in the kitchen we all shared, and occasionally going into town together. My welcoming, inquisitive, and often humorous flatmates made the semester a fantastic experience for me.

What does it mean to be a stranger in a foreign land? I was still in a country that shared English as the primary language, but now I was the one with an accent. For me, this was a healthy reminder that it is good to have the way we look at the world challenged. I'd often forget I "had an accent" until we would go out, and the waiter would be the one to say something or ask where I was from. My favorite story is when my mom came to visit me, and my flatmates were comparing our accents. I don't remember which of us had the stronger accent, but to my flatmates' ears, one of us definitely did! I also learned about how other voices sound to me and realized how distinct the different accents are within England. As each of the five flatmates I regularly spent time with was from a different part of England, they each had a slightly different accent. I could understand them all if I was talking to just one, but I remember one day two of them were trying to talk to me at the same time, and my head just exploded. I didn't make out a word that either of them said, and had to ask them both to repeat it, one at a time. It was good to be reminded to be patient when speaking with people back home in the United States who may be from a different country or learning English, as I would have an accent to them. Being a foreigner is often a humbling experience.

My flatmates helped me to experience England as they experienced it. We went out together, to dinner and a movie, to brunch at a pub, and on one occasion, to a Norwich City Football Club match (that's soccer to those of us in the United States). Norwich is a small city, about two hundred thousand people, and most years they aren't in the Premiere League, but this match was intense! The fans were way more into the game than our fans at a basketball or baseball game, and probably just as much as at an NFL game (and I say this living and attending events in Philadelphia, where the fans are, to put it politely, intense). You would have thought it was a championship match with how much the fans were into the game, not a regular match between two mediocre teams. It was an experience to be there, and when Norwich lost, I knew I didn't want to be with my one flatmate who was a big Norwich fan on the ride back to campus!

Living abroad also meant that I learned about assumptions, and that just as some of the assumptions they had about people from the United States were not all accurate (of course some were), our assumptions about "others" are also probably often mistaken. It was during this semester I started drinking tea regularly—more on that later—and there were many a conversation in the kitchen over a cuppa. I went to England in January of 2007, a time when President George W. Bush had an incredibly low approval rating, yet it surprised my flatmates that not all Americans liked President Bush, and that some very distinctly did not like him. They hadn't expected that there were many Americans who were opposed to the wars in Iraq and Afghanistan. With the two flatmates who were in medical school, there were many conversations about our various health care systems, as well as how the insurance industry works and effects medicine in the United States. Through our conversations, we were able to break down points of view that often lump large groups of people together and learn more about one another's nuanced ways of seeing the world.

There was a lot about life in the United Kingdom that was different too. Some of it was just being in a new place, and some of it was being in a new country. UEA is outside of town, so I took the bus thirty minutes into town to go to the grocery store and quickly learned that the stores did not stay open as late as back in Tucson. On Sundays, the grocery store closed at 5:00 p.m. Food was packaged differently as well, and while there were certain things I missed or that were fairly different (i.e., peanut butter, ketchup, and marshmallows), there were other new things that were quite tasty (milk chocolate Digestives, Crunchy Nut cereal, and some very good, inexpensive Brie). Having grown up in Arizona, I missed eating Southwestern food, and when my mom came to visit, she brought stuff with her to make some for me and my flatmates. One of the things she made was a simple cheese quesadilla, but one of my flatmates thought this new food was "brilliant." Being in a foreign land was a weird experience in some ways for me spiritually. I only went to church a handful of times and was significantly younger than anyone else there. I knew for a few months this would be okay but wondered what I would have done had I been there for longer. Classes were different, too, as was the grading system. I only had three classes; each met once a week for three hours, and we read about a book each week for each class (they were English literature classes). The way they fell in my weekly schedule made it easier to travel for long weekends, as well as to explore the area.

One of the things I loved about Norwich was how old the town was! Having grown up in Phoenix where very few things are even one hundred years old, this was incredibly different for me. In Norwich, the cathedral and castle had both been built only a few years after William the Conqueror arrived in England in 1066. I went to worship at the cathedral a few times and thought about how over nine hundred years' worth of baptisms, weddings, and funerals had occurred in this space. Elm Hill is a street in Norwich with buildings dating from the Tudor period, nearly five hundred years old, some of which have shops and cafes still. I'd take my reading and go find a spot in town to get tea and a scone, and just take everything in.

You're Not the Only One

Studying abroad also helped me to realize that, in many ways, the world is simultaneously a large and a very small place. This happened through the connections and similarities I found with those who I met there, but it also happened in a very specific way. One of my trips was to Orkney, an island of the northern coast of Scotland, that has lots of incredible Neolithic sites. To get to Orkney, you go to John O'Groats, and then take a ferry to the island. John O'Groats is literally in the middle of nowhere, a tiny town on the northern coast of Scotland. There's a small museum at the waiting area, and the friend who I was traveling with and I went in to look around while we waited for the ferry. While we were there, someone else came in and started looking around. I don't remember what exactly I was telling my friend, but the third person heard me mention University of Arizona and asked if I went there. He had graduated from U of A two years before, and now was living and working in London. Here I was thousands of miles from where I went to school as well as from the United States, running into another Wildcat in the middle of nowhere. He ended up spending time with us over the next few days as we explored Orkney. You never know who you'll meet, even across the world.

While in many ways I was in a foreign land, I was also in the land of some of my ancestors, and there were many things about the culture, the way of life, and even the ancient history, that resonated with me on a deeper level. It was during this semester that I developed the habit of drinking tea every morning, which was probably because I arrived in January and needed a kick-start since I was up long before the sun (not true in Arizona). I enjoyed the way that tea is a part of the culture as well, and how even when you went to office hours your professor might offer you a cup of tea when you arrived. The pace of life didn't seem as harried, and I truly enjoyed living there. I also cannot help but wonder about my fascination and connection to the Neolithic sites of Great Britain and Ireland, and what it is about them that I connect with so deeply. My ethnic heritage comes from a number of European countries, including England, Scotland, and Ireland, and I wonder if these ancient people were my ancestors and if their spiritual quest is in some ways continued millennia later in my own quest today.

The Scripture passage at the beginning of this chapter comes from the Levitical law code, and I know it's dangerous to go picking and choosing from that. I feel confident lifting up the passage, however, because it is echoed in Jesus' own teachings, as when Jesus talks about being a stranger and being welcomed in Matt 25. The Israelites are frequently reminded that they were once foreigners in the land of Egypt and to remember their history in how they treat foreigners. Traveling to a new and different place, whether that place is an hour from where you live or on the other side of the world, can be a good learning experience for us and remind us of what hospitality means and looks like. When we are the stranger, we look for that welcome, but need to remember to show it to others as well. When we welcome the stranger, we also open up opportunities for us to learn and grow and connect with people who can help expand our own worldview as well.

While I loved studying abroad and would highly recommend it, I also have to admit you are right if you worry that you will miss out on things that happen back home. I intentionally went abroad in spring so I wouldn't miss a marching band season, as I knew that was important to me. I was gone for five months, and had a different, often minimal experience of events that happened in the United States during that time. The shooting at Virginia Tech occurred that semester, and while I knew it happened, I think I would have experienced it differently had I been in the United States. I missed a semester of cultural references. There is a small assortment of pop songs that are missing from my repertoire, and when I can't place a song at all, it's often because it came out while I was abroad. There are also things you can't prepare for involving your relationships, such as one of your best friends and housemates meeting and starting to date the guy she is now married to. By the time I went back to Tucson after the summer, they had been together for over half a year. She and I had definitely been in touch while I was gone, but it was different than being there. I missed the giddy phase of the relationship, when things are new and exciting, and this made me feel like I had missed witnessing an important part of their relationship. My friends also had new inside jokes I wasn't inside of, memories made while I was five thousand miles away. Even though there were these things I missed out on or experienced differently, I wouldn't change going abroad.

Studying abroad is something that takes planning. Often, the further ahead you plan the less it will cost, and the more flexibility you will have with your course requirements. If it is something you have the opportunity to participate in, whether for a summer, semester, or year, it can be an important experience and learning opportunity. It provides you with a new perspective, a perspective that reshapes how you look at things when you return. This is something I see with many of the students at the CA who study abroad, who have gone to places all over the world. They often come back with a different understanding of themselves, as well as of our global community. Even if you can't study abroad, you can find ways to immerse yourself in a culture different from your own, in a place you feel like a stranger, and allow God to teach you through those experiences. We also can remember that we are called to always welcome the stranger in your community and show them God's love and hospitality.

Prayer

God,
You call us to remember when we were foreigners,
And to welcome the stranger among us.
Help us allow you to push us beyond our comfort zones,
To new places and new things,
To spaces in which we are the stranger.
Thank you for the hospitality of others,
For conversations that allow us to move beyond our assumptions,
For the times that remind us the world is broad,
Richly diverse,
And not centered around us and our way of life.
We pray this in the name of your son,
Who ministered to the stranger,
Amen.

Reflection Questions

1. When is a time you have felt like a stranger or foreigner? How were you received? What did this teach you?

2. What assumptions do you think people may have about the country you live in? Are these actually true, or not? What assumptions do you hold that may need to be challenged?

3. What does the Bible teach us about how we are supposed to treat the immigrant and the stranger? Is this a part of your faith that you live out? How should our faith perspective speak into our political perspective on this?

19

Engaging with People Who Are Different than You

> We are made for goodness. We are made for love. We are made for friendliness. We are made for togetherness. We are made for all of the beautiful things that you and I know. We are made to tell the world that there are no outsiders. All are welcome: black, white, red, yellow, rich, poor, educated, not educated, male, female, gay, straight, all, all, all. We all belong to this family, this human family, God's family.
>
> —Archbishop Desmond Tutu

> What I do believe . . . is that we are all somehow connected. Maybe there is a piece of God inside each of us, no matter what our religion, uniting us to our Divine Creator. Maybe this is a part of what Christians call the Holy Spirit.
>
> —My Thesis Journal

Scripture

For just as the body is one and has many members, and all the members of the body, though many, are one body, so it is with Christ. For in the one Spirit we were all baptized into one body—Jews or Greeks, slaves or free—and we were all made to drink of one Spirit.

Indeed, the body does not consist of one member but of many. If the foot would say, "Because I am not a hand, I do not belong to the body," that would not make it any less a part of the body. And if the ear would say, "Because I am not an eye, I do not belong to the body," that would not make it any less a part of the body. If the whole body were an eye, where would the hearing be? If the whole body were hearing, where would the sense of smell be? But as it is, God arranged the members in the body, each one of them, as he chose. If all were a single member, where would the body be? As it is, there are many members, yet one body. The eye cannot say to the hand, "I have no need of you," nor again the head to the feet, "I have no need of you." On the contrary, the members of the body that seem to be weaker are indispensable, and those members of the body that we think less honorable we clothe with greater honor, and our less respectable members are treated with greater respect; whereas our more respectable members do not need this. But God has so arranged the body, giving the greater honor to the inferior member, that there may be no dissension within the body, but the members may have the same care for one another. If one member suffers, all suffer together with it; if one member is honored, all rejoice together with it.

Now you are the body of Christ and individually members of it. (1 Cor 12:12–27)

UNLESS YOU HAVE MOVED a lot growing up, or lived in a foreign country, or been a part of an especially diverse community, chances are that before you go to college, you've been around a lot of people who are very similar to you. Even though you may have different interests in high school than your friends, everyone basically take the same classes, so you aren't even studying different things. Your friends are often involved in the same extracurriculars you are. There was some diversity in my group of friends in high school, but not nearly what I would experience when I went to college.

Often, once you arrive at college, engaging with people who are different from you is not really an option. It's bound to happen given the nature of higher education, though can be impacted by where you go to school. Generally, colleges and universities, and to some extant even community colleges, pull from a wider geographic area than your high school likely did. Many even have significant international student populations. You are likely to encounter people in your dorm, classes, extracurriculars, etc., who you might not otherwise have sought out.

As you arrive on campus your first year, one of the things that may be occupying a lot of your thoughts is what will your roommate be like and will you get along. Most likely, you'll be sharing a very small room with

Engaging with People Who Are Different than You

someone who may be very different than you, potentially in a multitude of ways. My freshman roommate and I got along just fine, although our lifestyles and interests were dissimilar in a number of ways. We kept very different schedules (which probably helped us get along better!). I was an academically focused freshman who spent my time studying, at marching band, at campus ministry, and sometimes volunteering. Katie pledged Theta, went to class in pajama pants a decent amount of the time, stayed up talking to her boyfriend on the phone until 3:00 a.m. most nights (she was considerate enough to go sit in the hall once I went to bed between 11:00 p.m. and midnight), and had a GPA that probably looked quite different than mine, which she was fine with. She liked to go out and have fun and then sleep in; I'm an early-to-bed, early-to-rise kind of girl. In college, I watched *The West Wing*; she watched reality shows. I wanted a German Shepherd mix I'd adopt from a shelter, she wanted a Pomeranian. I made my bed each day; her bed was often unmade with clothes on it. Overall, Katie and I had different personalities and liked different things, and we got along just fine. At the same time, aside from learning how to successfully share our room, we had similar enough backgrounds that she was not someone who challenged me to know someone who had lived a life that look very different from my own.

There were other places I would meet people who were more dissimilar to me. One of the things I loved about the Campus Christian Center being the space for multiple groups is that when I went to hang out or study there, I would likely get to interact with students from some of these other groups. Over the years I got to know some of them quite well. Our marching band was close to two hundred members, and I met many people there. The band included people from a lot of different backgrounds and a wide range of socioeconomic groups and was where I encountered the most students putting themselves through college without any help. Dr. Swaim and her classes drew students from a broad spectrum. This included some athletes as she served as an athletic advisor, as well as people of different faith traditions and all walks of life. We all met, however, in school, which meant that we still shared a similar level of education.

Once I had a car down at school, I started volunteering every Friday with an organization I think Pastor Ben first connected me with that got me out of my comfort zone. Here, I got to know others who had very different stories than my own. The Casa Maria Soup Kitchen, which is part of the Catholic Worker Movement, serves those experiencing housing and food insecurity. I would go help in the kitchen, often making sandwiches for them to hand out in lunch bags. I got to know the kitchen staff well and developed relationships with them. I never signed up to volunteer; it was just a show-up kind of deal, and if there was a week I had something due or a test and didn't make it, they would express concern when they saw me the next week. I learned how to comfortably interact with those outside who were waiting for the meals to be served, the vast majority of whom were experiencing homelessness, and became aware of our shared humanity and the need for connection. It was experiences like these, along with my sense of connection to the people who had lived five thousand years prior in Neolithic England that led me to the write the following in my senior thesis: "This leads me to the realization that we are all connected, across space and time. No matter how individual we think we are, we cannot escape that we are a part of the great story of humanity. Nor can we escape that we are all dependent upon one another."[1]

As we embrace that we are all dependent on one another, it can mean that we are called to do things that we may not have expected or that may not even always feel comfortable for us. It is not uncommon for us as Christians to be called on to not only engage, but also build relationships with people who are different from us, including those who have other belief systems. In *Velvet Elvis*, Rob Bell writes, "If you come across truth in any form, it isn't outside your faith as a Christian. Your faith just got bigger. To be a Christian is to claim truth wherever you find it."[2] I believe that there is a lot of truth I can learn from my neighbors of different faiths, just as, hopefully, there are things that I can offer as well. From my Jewish neighbors, I have learned the importance of lament, and I have witnessed practices around death and grieving that I think we all can learn from. I've also learned other ways of engaging with Scripture that create space for imagination and questions. From my Muslim neighbors, I have learned what it looks like to have life-shaping dedication to prayer, and I know if I had such dedication it would have a rich impact on my relationship with God. From my Indigenous neighbors I have witnessed a respect for and connection with all of creation, especially nature and all life, that I believe bears witness to how we were meant to live in relation with the earth and all its creatures. I could go on and on.

---

1. LeCluyse, "To Think of Time," 24.
2. Bell, *Velvet Elvis*, 81.

Engaging with People Who Are Different than You

During my second year at the CA, I got to see what it looks like to learn from one another play out in a special way. In the fall of 2013, several incidents occurred that led to the CA hosting a series of dialogues with the Penn Secular Society (PSS), a student group that described itself as being for those who were irreligious. One of our grad students, Geeta, was particularly involved in orchestrating this. Here is an excerpt from a blog she wrote for the CA as these events were unfolding. For this story to make sense, you need to know that Locust Walk forms the middle line of Penn's campus and is the main thoroughfare for pedestrians through campus. Over a stretch of about 250 feet, there are spots that can be reserved on either side of the walk for a student organization to hang a banner. She wrote the piece interspersed with the lyrics from "They Will Know We Are Christians by Our Love."

> In the first two weeks of November, Penn Secular Society posted two banners. The first had a list of names of deities from various myths and legends—Hera, Odin, and the like—that most people no longer believe in and asked Penn's campus the question, "What's one more?" Within hours, parts of the list had been torn down and soup and coffee had been thrown at the sign. The following week, their banner posted 3 verses that present evidence that women should not be welcome in the Church or in public spaces: Deuteronomy 22:23–24, 1 Timothy 2:12, and Surat An-Nisa' 4:34 from the Old Testament/Tanukh, New Testament, and Qur'an respectively. Within just 5 hours, it was defaced.
>
> Perhaps it is time to ask ourselves why we react so emotionally when our faith is questioned. Why we immediately become defensive and allow it to "ruin our day."[3] Why we revert to a vain attempt to defend the irrational . . . why people of religion feel the need to throw soup and coffee, and not so long ago stones, at people and ideas with which they disagree. And we all know what Christ said about stone throwing.
>
> Enough blood (and soup) has been spilled in the name of a God who spoke of peace and love. Perhaps it is time to move beyond praying for unity and moving towards dialogue.
>
> The Secular Society asked people to respond to their banners by posting on their Facebook group, attending their meetings, and having these conversations that are incredibly terrifying but equally necessary. I encourage people of faith to engage. If people

---

3. The phrase "ruin our day" is a reference to a quote from a student in an article that ran in *The Daily Pennsylvanian*, covering the story of what happened to the banner.

are knocking on our doors and seeking answers, then isn't it our duty to respond?[4]

This blog was posted on November 12, and around that time, Geeta and others started planning a coffee chat for the first Saturday in December. It was great and brought in people of other faiths as well. We all learned a lot about one another, including some of those who belonged to PSS realizing that there were Christians who were welcoming of the LGBTQ+ community. Several more of these coffee chats were held that spring, and another the following fall. At these gatherings, people of incredibly different belief systems engaged in real dialogue, by and large really seeking to learn from one another and not to prove each other right or wrong. People brought curiosity, and it was a powerful experience.

It seems like the CA has a long history of bringing together students of diverse backgrounds, which has been wonderful to be part of. From what I have seen, it's a place that brings together students of different races, ethnicities, cultures, socioeconomic classes, gender identities, and sexuality, and while the vast majority are Christian, they come from a wide array of Christian backgrounds. They are also studying an incredible range of subjects, including multiple facets of business like economics, marketing, ethics, and statistics, nursing, bioengineering, criminology, urban studies, theater, education, public policy, and so many more. It's a space where students are encouraged to be who they are and are also given the space to ask questions of others in a safe way. Working in this environment means that I, too, am constantly learning and growing!

We often hear this well-known passage from 1 Corinthians used to talk about how we are all important to the body of Christ or how we all have different gifts, but there is so much more to it than just that. When you think about the different parts of our body, they have vastly different functions, which often don't even resemble each other. The eye takes in the outside world and creates a visual understanding of what surrounds us, while our feet support our bodies when we stand and work with our legs to give us mobility, while the pancreas controls our blood sugar to make sure that it is at a proper level, and the appendix, well, we don't even know what that one is there for (and mine was removed when I was an infant)! This passage is inviting us to realize how vital it is that we aren't all the same because we need a community comprised of something that resembles the 206 bones, 650 muscles, 9 systems, 22 internal organs, and roughly 100

---

4. Aneja, "By Our Love."

trillion cells that make up the human body. And while the passage is talking about the body of Christ, if we believe that every person is a child of God, then I think this also represents that body of humanity as well.

One of the beautiful things about Martin Buber's concept of "I and Thou" relationships that we discussed in one of Dr. Swaim's classes is that none of these differences matter.[5] It is a moment of transcendence in which souls connect, and it doesn't matter whether one is this, that, or the other. When we again become aware of the things that identify us, we might marvel at the shared moment. When we engage with others who are different from ourselves, it helps us to grow personally and learn more about ourselves, but it also broadens our horizons and helps us break out of some of the boxes we have created. It also pushes us toward a realization that we are all humans, all children of God, deserving of dignity and respect, with a lot to offer each other.

Prayer

Wondrous God,
Who made so much diversity within our world,
Thank you for this time when we have the opportunity
To seek out relationships with peers who are different from us,
In any and in every way.
Help us to not fear the things that seem unfamiliar,
But to be open and curious,
Ready to listen but also to share.
Allow our worldview to change.
Call us in to new places and relationships,
To be a friend and conversation partner,
And to give thanks for all the many parts of the body,
Each with their own role and function,
All of which are needed to make the body work as it should.
Amen.

---

5. Martin Buber describes "I and Thou" and "I and It" relationships. Anytime we assign an identity to someone, we have made them an "it," and it is only in rare moments that we experience "I and Thou" connections. A fuller description of this can be found in chapter 10.

You're Not the Only One

REFLECTION QUESTIONS

1. Have you ever become close with someone who was fairly different from you in some way? What did you learn from that person? Did they open you to new ideas?

2. What role do you think you play in the body? What kind of things are you really good at? What kind of "functions" do you know that you need others to do? How many different types of people do we need to make our normal lives work?

3. What would be a way you could continue to develop new relationships that will help you grow?

20

Why Do Bad Things Happen to Good People?

Faith does not mean certainty. It means the courage to live with uncertainty. It does not mean having the answers, it means having the courage to ask the questions and not let go of God, as he does not let go of us. It means realizing that God creates divine justice but only we, acting in accord with his word, can create human justice—and our very existence means that this is what God wants us to do. For one who sets a hard challenge does not do so to punish, but because he believes in the one to whom he sets the challenge. At the heart of [God's] call to responsibility . . . is God's unshakable faith in humankind.

—Rabbi Jonathan Sacks

Have patience with everything that remains unsolved in your heart. Try to love the *questions themselves*, like locked rooms and like books written in a foreign language. Do not now look for the answers. They cannot now be given to you because you could not live them. It is a question of experiencing everything. At present you need to *live* the question. Perhaps you will gradually, without even noticing it, find yourself experiencing the answer, some distant day.

—Rainer Maria Rilke

Scripture

My God, my God, why have you forsaken me?
Why are you so far from helping me, from the words of my groaning?

You're Not the Only One

O my God, I cry by day, but you do not answer;
and by night, but find no rest. . . .
The Lord is my shepherd, I shall not want.
He makes me lie down in green pastures;
he leads me beside still waters;
he restores my soul.
He leads me in right paths
for his name's sake.
Even though I walk through the darkest valley,
I fear no evil;
for you are with me;
your rod and your staff,
they comfort me.
You prepare a table before me
in the presence of my enemies;
you anoint my head with oil;
my cup overflows.
Surely goodness and mercy shall follow me
all the days of my life,
and I shall dwell in the house of the Lord
my whole life long.
(Ps 22:1–2; Ps 23)

So I say to you, Ask, and it will be given you; search, and you will find; knock, and the door will be opened for you. For everyone who asks receives, and everyone who searches finds, and for everyone who knocks, the door will be opened. Is there anyone among you who, if your child asks for a fish, will give a snake instead of a fish? Or if the child asks for an egg, will give a scorpion? If you then, who are evil, know how to give good gifts to your children, how much more will the heavenly Father give the Holy Spirit to those who ask him! (Luke 11:9–13)

DURING SPRING BREAK OF my sophomore year of college, a group of us from the PCM spent the week working with Presbyterian Disaster Assistance in New Orleans, Louisiana. It was just shy of seven months since the area had been devastated by Hurricane Katrina. In some ways, it was one of the emotionally harder service trips I have been a part of. It was still early on in the recovery from Katrina, and what we were doing was gutting houses. As humans, we like to build, to make progress, to feel as though we are moving forward. Gutting a house, literally tearing it apart, is counter intuitive. Going through a family's belongings, seeing what might

Why Do Bad Things Happen to Good People?

be salvaged and what is ruined, is tragic. You are standing in the midst of people's lives that have been shattered, on streets that were largely deserted because almost all of the homes were still uninhabitable. Neighborhoods were mostly empty; spray painted *X*s on houses showed you what had been found, including bodies of people or pets. At this point, there was still a chance some of the work we were doing was on houses that might ultimately be condemned, depending on how bad the damage uncovered turned out to be. Did the work we were doing matter? Why had God allowed this to happen, and for that matter, why does our planet seem to contain such volatility, with disasters impacting so many each year, even before we've made things worse through climate change? Where was God in the midst of what was happening now?

These are the kinds of questions we will find ourselves asking throughout life, questions that we never can fully feel like we have answers to. Things will happen in your own life, in the lives of people we love, even in the lives of strangers, and we really just want to scream and ask God, "Why?" Why do innocent children suffer because adults go to war? Why are there people hungry when there is enough food on the planet for all to be fed? Why did a friend die in a freak accident? There are plenty of times I still want to ask, "Why?" It's easy to get stuck there. It makes me think of the scene in *Star Wars: Episode V—The Empire Strikes Back* where Yoda says, "No, no, there is no why. Nothing more will I teach you today. Clear your mind of questions."[1]

People talk about how the way out of some things is through. Clearing our mind of the questions doesn't mean dismissing the questions; to me, it means figuring out what to do with them. It's not easy to clear our mind of questions, but there are two responses that are part of how we might move through them, and they are both centered around prayer. The first of these is through lamenting. It was not until seminary that I really understood the biblical concept of lament, even though close to half of Psalms contains lament. There is even a book of the Bible named after the practice (Lamentations), a book that laments the destruction of Jerusalem. Lament just wasn't something I really heard discussed growing up. Lament gives us permission to ask tough questions, to be angry at God, or what God has allowed to happen. Flip through Psalms, a book that I found myself coming back to again and again in 2020, a year of a lot of pain, injustice, and questioning why things were happening. Throughout Psalms there is

---

1. Kershner, *Star Wars*, 1:11.

some yelling, screaming, shaking-the-fist-at-God kind of talk going on, but lament is about more than just being angry, grief stricken, devastated. It is about acknowledging God's presence in this place of suffering.

There is a scene from the final episode of the second season of *The West Wing* that beautifully captures lament, though it comes with spoilers. President Bartlett, played by Martin Sheen, attends the funeral of his beloved secretary, Mrs. Landingham, who had been hit and killed by a drunk driver while returning home from buying her first ever, brand new car. Angry at God for this and a variety of other things occurring in his life, he remains after the funeral service ends and waits for the church to clear out. He then stands about halfway down the center aisle and lets loose as he walks forward to the front of the sanctuary. He rails at God about things that don't make sense, that have no explanation, asking if all that he has given hasn't been enough, and as he walks back down the center aisle, stops, and lights a cigarette, which he then drops and grounds out on the floor of the National Cathedral. Bartlett isn't so much saying "woe is me" as he is wondering why all this bad stuff can happen, and too often to people who are good and trying to do the right thing. We don't see the turn to praise that is typical in lament, but he chooses to engage with God and wrestle instead of rejecting God in his pain.

To me there is such freedom in knowing that we have been given the freedom to do this, the freedom to lament, to turn to God and just let loose with the assurance that God is going to listen, hear us, and be present, even if we let loose a string of profanities. Another thing I learned in seminary is that many biblical scholars think that what we now read as Pss 22 and 23 were originally coupled, that you wouldn't read one without reading the other. You may recognize the first words of Ps 22 as the words Jesus utters as he dies on the cross: "My God, my God, why have you forsaken me?" (Matt 24:46; Mark 15:34). Psalm 22 begins in a dark place. Like almost every other Psalm of lament, however, it turns, and shifts towards praise of God and all that God has done. Then it leads into Ps 23, a psalm that for many is one of the most familiar and comforting. Thousands of years ago, the psalmists were able to capture and put down on paper how emotionally conflicted we can feel, how we can feel such despair and God's overwhelming presence at the same time, how life can be a roller coaster or giant pot of emotions of which lament and praise are both important parts. It's also interesting to contemplate what Jesus meant when he spoke these words on the cross. His doing so would likely have brought all that the two psalms contain to the minds of those who heard him—the suffering, utter devastation, and physical brokenness of Ps 22 but also the hope and promise of Ps 23, words that may have felt unattainable as Jesus hung on the cross but a promise nonetheless.

The second response is prayer more broadly speaking. If you're like me, when you first read that passage from Luke, you probably balk. The Rev. Dr. Jana Childers, a Presbyterian minister and homiletics professor, writes in a sermon on this passage, "The gospel according to Luke is not easy to hear today, not easy to preach, because it is not easy to believe. 'Ask and it shall be given to you?!' How could Jesus have said such a thing? How can that be true?"[2] She goes on to point out that if we take it literally, as it is often translated into English, every eight-year-old girl would have her own pony. It turns out, the way we often read it in English, almost implying God is a magic genie who will grant you whatever wishes you make, is not actually a very good translation of the Greek. Childers writes, "The New Testament Greek does not say 'Ask and you will receive.' It says 'aaaaaask and keep on asking . . . seeeeeek and keep on seeking . . . knoooock and keep on knocking.' The Greek verb implies ongoing action. Be persistent, Jesus is saying. Be shameless. Run right up to that door and pound on it and keep on pounding on it. Make a fool out of yourself with your asking."[3]

This is a passage about prayer and about the power that prayer can have on us. Prayer is a relationship, it takes coming back to again and again. Prayer can be something you close your eyes, bow your head, and do, but it can also be an ongoing conversation you have with God, little things said throughout the day. Sometimes it is praise, sometimes it is lament, and sometimes prayer can just be chatting about whatever is going on in our lives and asking God for guidance in it all. It can happen as we walk, run, hike, swim, do yoga, or sit still. It can happen as we cook a meal, do dishes, or stare into space while working on homework. We need to also remember that prayer is meant to be a conversation, and unless you want to be one of those people who just never shuts up, that means making time to listen, too. Listening may not provide the exact answers or outcomes we were looking for, but it can help us see that we have been given what we truly need, which is to know that God is with us no matter what may come. Childers concludes her sermon by talking about how what we get may not look like what we hoped for, but what we get is, "God. The God who is nearer than hands

---

2. Childers, *Birthing the Sermon*, 46.
3. Childers, *Birthing the Sermon*, 47.

and feet. God's own presence is the answer to every prayer—the answer that surpasses anything we could ask for."[4]

I don't know why bad things happen to good people, and in this life, I don't think I ever will. But I do know that in almost the exact middle of the book of Lamentations, you find the following verses:

> The steadfast love of the Lord never ceases,
> his mercies never come to an end;
> they are new every morning;
> great is your faithfulness.
> "The Lord is my portion," says my soul,
> "therefore I will hope in him." (Lam 3:22–24)

God is present with us. God extends an invitation to lament, and God grieves with us. God does not ask us to put on a smile and pretend that everything is okay, to suck it up and push through. God invites us to be real, to let ourselves be vulnerable and put it all out there, and to do this again and again and again. We may not feel like we have gotten the answer we were looking for or even any answer, but we can keep asking. And we are promised that we are given God, a promise we see born out in Jesus, Immanuel, God with us (which is what Immanuel means). Not only did God come to live as a human, God suffered as a human. Jesus laughed with his friends, and he cried with his friends. He took the worst humanity offered—crucifixion—and through the resurrection showed that God has the last word (or words), and those words are life, love, grace, and hope.

Ask, seek, knock, lament, praise, or just pray. There is no right or wrong way to do it. It just matters that you make yourself present to the moment and allow room for God to be present with you. Some days this may help clear your mind of the questions. Other days, you may not feel quite there. No matter what, God promises to give us something good—God's presence with us—to walk with us even through the valley of the shadow of death.

Prayer

Holy one,
Our patient creator,
Thank you for giving us the example of the psalmists,
Who brought everything to you:
Joy, adoration, thanksgiving,

---

4. Childers, *Birthing the Sermon*, 49.

Along with anguish, sadness, anger, and confusion.
Allow me to bring all of myself before you in prayer,
And to come back to this space
Day after day, hour after hour.
Remind me that prayer isn't just about talking,
But is also about listening,
About allowing room to see where you are already at work
In our lives and in the world.
Thank you for your promise to be with us,
To stay by our side in times of struggle
As well as in times of happiness.
Remind us to pray for those we love and those unknown,
For in our prayers for one another,
We witness to your amazing love.
Amen.

Reflection Questions

1. How familiar are you with the concept of lament? If you have heard it talked about before, how was it discussed? If not, what are your initial thoughts about this form of prayer?

2. Have you ever lamented before? What might this practice look like for you? What forms could lament take that are not spoken or written word?

3. What are some of the prayer practices that you find meaningful? Are there any you would like to try out? How is prayer a conversation for you?

4. What does it mean to you to keep on asking, knocking, and seeking? How have you experienced God's response in your life?

21

Coming Face-to-Face with Mortality

> Now looking at the bigger picture, the most basic way in which every individual is connected to the human story is through their mortality.
>
> —Megan LeCluyse, "To Think of Time"

> Eternal life doesn't start when we die; it starts now. It's not about a life that begins at death; it's about experiencing the kind of life now that can endure and survive even death.
>
> —Rob Bell

Scripture

For the fate of humans and the fate of animals is the same; as one dies, so dies the other. They all have the same breath, and humans have no advantage over the animals; for all is vanity. All go to one place; all are from the dust, and all turn to dust again.
(Eccl 3:19–20)

When Mary came where Jesus was and saw him, she knelt at his feet and said to him, "Lord, if you had been here, my brother would not have died." When Jesus saw her weeping, and the Jews who came with her also weeping, he was greatly disturbed in spirit and deeply moved. He said, "Where have you laid him?" They said to him, "Lord, come and see." Jesus began to weep. So the Jews said, "See how he loved him!" (Luke 11:32–36)

Coming Face-to-Face with Mortality

I KNOW THIS SEEMS like a morbid title and topic, but I've always had what some people find to be an uncanny comfort in talking about mortality and death. I'll listen to shows on NPR, in which they are constantly giving listeners reminders that they are talking about death, sharing that this is a sensitive topic for some in case they want to change the station. Meanwhile, it simultaneously fascinates and disturbs me that talking about human mortality is so hard for us. Some of you will get why this chapter is here, because you have already had some experience that has made you fully aware of your own mortality. Others might skip this chapter now but come back at some point during your college experience when this happens and you are trying to figure out how to process it. Others may not experience this until later, or intentionally push it away and choose not to deal with it. Once you have had an experience that forces you to confront your mortality, you will feel different from those who have not. The way you see the world and the value you place on life shifts. It's not that you won't take risks anymore; you will, but you understand risk and the choices you make in a different way.

I became fully aware of my own morality and the fragility of life when I was twelve. My family was in an eleven-car pileup about sixty miles after leaving our home in Phoenix for a road trip to see family in the Midwest. Two people were killed, and close to twenty others were injured. There was a body pinned under the car behind us, which I knew was there but chose not to look at. We were in one of two cars from which no one went to the hospital. Annie, my sister, was nine at the time. Her memories are very different than mine and our parents, and while still a traumatic event, the two-and-a-half-year age difference played a developmental role here in how we each processed the accident.

Her realization of her mortality happened the summer before her senior year of college. Annie and I spent the summer of 2009 living with our cousin in Arlington, VA, and both had internships in Washington, DC. Annie's was at the United States Holocaust Memorial Museum. She was working on the fourth floor on June 10, the day that a white supremacist shot Museum Special Police Officer Stephen Tyrone Johns, who died at the hospital that afternoon from his injuries. Annie went through the evacuation procedure, escorting guests out of the building, knowing that this was not a drill. Annie had not known Stephen especially well, but he was someone she would say hello to on her way into the museum each morning, someone whose smile she counted on to start her day. His murder, and sudden absence from the front door, was when she became aware of her own mortality. Unlike our elderly grandparents, who had passed away while Annie was in middle and high school, Stephen was only thirty-nine years old, had a young child, and was not someone who was expected to die. When she returned to school that fall, she felt like she viewed life differently from her peers and found that the summer had changed her in a way that it had not changed her friends. She felt different in the way I had felt different since the car accident. You value life more, realize how precious each day is, but also are more aware of our fragility. You have an awareness of how what you expected to always be, or who you expected to see or talk to, can suddenly vanish. Living with this awareness when those around you don't seem to have it can feel very lonely.

It is not uncommon for us to have some type of experience where we are forced to confront our own mortality during college or young adulthood. One of my former students, Nick, reached out about a year after he graduated, when he found himself struggling to process the death of two of his former classmates that occurred about a month apart. Nick's father had passed away during his senior year at Penn, so he had experienced the death of a loved one, but not someone his same age. Now, within a couple of weeks, two people Nick's own age had died. He wrote me in an email,

> On another note, I was wondering if I could seek your pastoral advice. Recently I've been struggling in my faith, having had two acquaintances pass away tragically. I knew one person from my time at Penn, and the other was someone I didn't know personally but most likely had classes with during my time at [my prior university]. Still, their deaths hit close to home, especially because one occurred violently on the Metro train that I travel on quite frequently. I've been praying a lot, but I find myself caught back in a state of lament, wondering why God allows such horrible things to happen to young, intelligent, vibrant people. I find myself not only grieving for them, but also worried that something similar could happen to me. I know we are not to understand God's motives, but it's such a struggle sometimes to enjoy the present for what it is when the future is never guaranteed. I know you don't have all the answers, and this rant was mainly for cathartic purposes, but any advice you have would be greatly appreciated.[1]

Both of these deaths were unexpected and unusual. The one of his classmate from the school he had attended his freshman year had been the result of a random act of violence and murder on a subway train. A clear

---

1. Email message to author, July 8, 2015.

motive never was fully understood, but the attack was concluded to be a consequence of the perpetrator being under the influence of drugs. The death of his classmate from Penn was a young person who developed an unusual infection of the pericardium that ultimately was fatal and that no one saw coming. It was completely expected that Nick would be both grieving and thinking that either of these young people could have been him. I felt I needed to respond both to his grief, and to the sense of vulnerability he was expressing:

> As for the pastoral piece . . . [t]he death of young people tends to always be especially hard. Both of these deaths also seem totally random. If the death at Penn is the one I know of, it's not normal for a twenty-three-year-old to get sick and die in two weeks like that. And the metro one is crazy! It makes total sense for it to freak you out. . . . it makes sense that in the midst of your grief you are worrying that something could happen to you. I know this may sound like a weird question—but have you had an experience before that made you feel aware of your own mortality? It sounds like this might be that experience for you. . . . When you have this experience, it is life-changing, if you are willing to work through it, and not run from it. It changes how you understand life. But in a culture that doesn't like to deal with or talk about death, it can also feel weird. The way I talk about my own mortality freaks people out! If I remember right—you are one of those people who it freaked out when you heard I have planned my own funeral (for a class project) :)
>
> So that's one side—and then there is the God piece. You're right, I don't have answers. Except I firmly believe that these bright, promising young people dying is not the will of God. I don't think God caused it, and I think God laments it too. Did it happen for a reason—well sure, if you want to call disease and a culture of violence and synthetic drugs reasons. So I think lament is good, and I think God laments at how broken our world is, and how often we as people have chosen sin over good. Allow yourself to feel what you feel, and to ask the tough questions that you have. This isn't fair—and we can say that. It's tragic, and messed up. And yes, scary, because it could be us. Which may not feel helpful for me to say—but believe it is possible to know that you are mortal and still be happy and enjoy living life to the fullest! But if this is that experience for you [of realizing your own mortality], it's really hard in the beginning.

A little while later, Nick responded:

> I think your description of it being a first "realizing my own mortality" moment was completely accurate. When I lost my Dad, I became aware of mortality as a real and present entity, but those somewhat recent experiences emphasized my own mortality on a personal level. You're right, it is super scary and awful. But it does make you count your blessings and in my case, brought me closer to God, even if it was to lament the loss of two young, bright lives.[2]

Although it can be painful, scary, and tough, I still contend that an awareness of our mortality, our vulnerability, our fragility, is a good thing. Interestingly, so does the church calendar. We have a day in our church calendar for the purpose of humbling us with a reminder of our own mortality, our fragility. Ash Wednesday, the beginning of the season of Lent, is marked in some denominations by the imposition of ashes. The pastor makes the sign of the cross on one's forehead with ashes (often made by burning the palms from Palm Sunday the prior year). As the sign of the cross is made, the verse from Ecclesiastes is paraphrased: "From dust you came, to dust you shall return." Over the years, as we've joined with partner congregations for this service, I am especially struck when I make the sign of the cross for an elderly person, whose mortality is visibly present in their aging body, and on children, who I wish were not as vulnerable as they are. Imposing ashes onto the students' foreheads or hands that I work with is also a strange experience, to be reminded that these strong, healthy young people are also mortal. This day is solemn, but not something to be dreaded. It begins a season of inner examination or simplifying your life to focus on the spiritual. It is an invitation.

While I appreciate Ash Wednesday and what it does for us, I believe that we need to be aware of our mortality other days of the year too. As I explored the lives of the Neolithic people of Great Britain in my senior thesis, I wrote the following:

> Today I often feel as if we are taught to fear death. I have been a part of discussions, however, about how realizing our mortality actually allows us to live more fully. The Neolithic people seemed to embrace their mortality. The people of these sites seem to have made symbols of death a part of their daily lives; the tombs they built were highly visible and often seem to have been near the village. They built monuments that were about death, where they would honor their ancestors.[3]

2. Facebook direct message to author, September 16, 2015.
3. LeCluyse, "To Think of Time," 20.

Coming Face-to-Face with Mortality

We live in a time in which we have tried to remove death from our lives—both in the sense of no longer having coffins in homes after a family member dies and in the sense of technological advances meant to extend, and some hope eventually prevent, death. I love what Dumbledore tells Harry, though, when Harry is concerned that destroying the Sorcerer's Stone will cause Nicolas Flamel to finally die: "To the well-organized mind, death is but the next great adventure."[4]

I love what he says because this is in fact what we believe. We believe there is something wonderful for us after this life—a life with God. I don't know what exactly I think heaven looks like or feels like, but I know it will be clear that we are with God and enmeshed into God's love. I also take comfort in knowing Jesus knew and experienced death. Jesus mourns the loss of his friend Lazarus, as well as others. God knows what it feels like to grieve. God also experienced death. This really, truly means that there is nowhere that we can go that God cannot go or has not been.

We were created to live beautiful, meaningful lives, and this means not letting ourselves be consumed with fear. That said, this is a huge topic, and it is not uncommon for the event that triggers our awareness of our mortality to be traumatic. Seek out the people and support that you need during this time. Talk to a trusted family member, pastor, mentor, or therapist. If someone especially close to you has died, many counseling centers also have grief support groups that might help you find a place to connect with other students going through a similar experience. As I said in the quote from my thesis at the beginning of this chapter, our mortality is one thing we all have in common. Don't try to go through this experience alone.

We are indeed human, fragile, mortal. May we see each day as the precious gift that it is. May we remember that when God cares so tenderly for the flowers and the birds, God will care for us, too, both in this life and the next.

Prayer

God of life and death,
It is hard to face the unknown,
To realize that each day is not a guarantee,
But a precious gift.
Be with us when we become all too aware

---

4. Rowling, *Sorcerer's Stone*, 297.

You're Not the Only One

Of our own mortality,
How fragile life can be.
Remind us that you, too,
Lament the brokenness of our world,
The loss of young people whose lives are cut short,
The loneliness we feel when we lose those who lived long lives.
Remind us that you have also grieved,
That you have experienced death,
And that you have promised us a future with you,
Where we are united,
And death and pain are no more.
Amen.

REFLECTION QUESTIONS

1. Has something happened in your life that has made you feel aware of your own mortality? Do you feel comfortable talking about what this was? How did it change your outlook on life?

2. What do you imagine heaven to be like? What is important to you about how heaven will be? Why?

3. Why do Jesus' experiences with death matter? What do they mean to you?

22

Connecting Across Space and Time
We Are a Part of a Bigger Story

Life is not about being correct but about being connected.
At all costs, stay connected!

—Richard Rohr

Only connect! That was the whole of her sermon.

—E. M. Forster[1]

If I were to try and sum it up, I would have to say that what draws me to these sites and the people who built them was realizing my connection to them as part of the human story.

—Megan LeCluyse, "To Think of Time"

Scripture

Moses was keeping the flock of his father-in-law Jethro, the priest of Midian; he led his flock beyond the wilderness, and came to Horeb, the mountain of God. There the angel of the Lord appeared to him in a flame of fire out of a bush; he looked, and the bush was blazing, yet it was not consumed. Then Moses said, "I must turn aside and look at this great sight, and see why the bush is not

---

1. *Howard's End* was one of the books we read for the first semester I took Spirituality in the Arts with Prof. Swaim.

burned up." When the Lord saw that he had turned aside to see, God called to him out of the bush, "Moses, Moses!" And he said, "Here I am." Then he said, "Come no closer! Remove the sandals from your feet, for the place on which you are standing is holy ground." He said further, "I am the God of your father, the God of Abraham, the God of Isaac, and the God of Jacob." And Moses hid his face, for he was afraid to look at God.

Then the Lord said, "I have observed the misery of my people who are in Egypt; I have heard their cry on account of their taskmasters. Indeed, I know their sufferings, and I have come down to deliver them from the Egyptians, and to bring them up out of that land to a good and broad land, a land flowing with milk and honey, to the country of the Canaanites, the Hittites, the Amorites, the Perizzites, the Hivites, and the Jebusites. The cry of the Israelites has now come to me; I have also seen how the Egyptians oppress them. So come, I will send you to Pharaoh to bring my people, the Israelites, out of Egypt." But Moses said to God, "Who am I that I should go to Pharaoh, and bring the Israelites out of Egypt?" He said, "I will be with you; and this shall be the sign for you that it is I who sent you: when you have brought the people out of Egypt, you shall worship God on this mountain."

But Moses said to God, "If I come to the Israelites and say to them, 'The God of your ancestors has sent me to you,' and they ask me, 'What is his name?' what shall I say to them?" God said to Moses, "I am who I am." He said further, "Thus you shall say to the Israelites, 'I am has sent me to you.'" God also said to Moses, "Thus you shall say to the Israelites, 'The Lord, the God of your ancestors, the God of Abraham, the God of Isaac, and the God of Jacob, has sent me to you':

This is my name forever, and this my title for all generations." (Exod 3:1–15)

I FIRST SAW STONEHENGE when I was fourteen and was fascinated by it. It created so many questions for me. If aliens didn't build it (one of the more humorous suggestions offered by the tourist headset you walked around with), then how was it built, and why? My parents gave me books about Stonehenge for Christmas, and my family just kind of accepted it was a peculiar interest of mine. The interest grew. When my cousin studied abroad in Scotland during my freshman year of college, I decided to go visit her. I asked Dr. Swaim where we should travel to, and she told me that we should go to Orkney. She had never been, but it was on her list of places she wanted to go. Orkney is an island to the north of Scotland, on which there are a number of Neolithic sites, including stone circles, a passage tomb, and a five-thousand-year-old village that lay hidden under sand until the mid-nineteenth century. Mae's How, the passage tomb, was incredible. On the winter solstice (and for several days on either side), the setting sun shines straight down the passage, and creates a golden door on the back wall of the tomb. While we can't know exactly what this meant to its builders, the symbolism points to rebirth, in life as the days started getting longer and the sun would be able to help crops grow, and potentially in death as well, as the door was created on the back wall of a tomb, potentially signifying a door to whatever lies beyond this life. This would have likely taken them years to build, pointing towards its significance in their society. The Ring of Brodgar, the stone circle, is about the length of a football field in diameter, and it's one degree off of a perfect circle. I still get excited thinking and talking about these places and what they have to tell us.

By the time I went to study abroad during my junior year, I knew I wanted to write my thesis on the Neolithic sites of Great Britain. What I had not yet figured out was that one of my foci would be the role these sites played for me and for my own journey. It's hard to describe, but something about these sites resonates deeply for me. I feel a connection to them, to the people who lived there, to the things they may have sought after in life. In September of my senior year, I wrote in my thesis journal, "What is it that calls me personally to prehistoric British sites? Ultimately, I am not entirely sure. It is just some[thing] that has taken hold of me; spoken to me across the ages if you will." At first, this felt weird to me; after all, we would call these people pagans. We don't know if they had gods or not, or if they worshiped the forces of nature such as the sun and the rain. As a college student who knew I wanted to be a pastor, it freaked me out that I would feel such a strong connection to these people we would call not only pagan but primitive. As I learned about them, I felt that we weren't actually all that different. As the year progressed, the thesis not only researched the Neolithic sites but also explored the role that they played in my own spiritual journey.

In my thesis, I reflected on this sense of shared connection and the ways in which we connect to the broader story of humanity as I reflected on an event that took place my senior year:

> What, in part, intrigued me so much about these places were the similarities that I shared with these people. Realizing that humans have probably changed very little in terms of our basic needs and

emotions for over five thousand years is incredibly powerful. One night this past September, we had worship for Presbyterian Campus Ministry on the roof of the building we meet in. As I lay on my back, I looked at the stars, thinking about how the stars have barely changed in the relatively short time span of five thousand years. The stars I saw were about the same stars the Neolithic people saw. When worship finished, I stayed on the roof with one of my friends, who was going through a difficult period of her life. We sat on the roof together, leaning into each other, as she sobbed. Underneath the stars sat two young women helping each other to deal with the challenges of life. Somehow, I felt that the same exact thing probably happened around the dying embers of a fire millennia ago. As I realized that this is part of what drew me to the sites, I also began to better understand what the human story is, and also found myself in the midst of a personal journey.[2]

My friend's parents were getting a divorce, and her heart was breaking. While divorce may or may not have happened in these Neolithic societies, I know heartache did. Sitting beneath the stars, I felt that five thousand years is really not much time at all in the course of the universe, and I realized some of the ways that we as humans are so deeply connected through the human experience across space and time.

I realized that I felt the connections of grief, of community, of sharing experiences together. The story of humanity, the story of being human, means that we are a part of something that is beyond our individual selves. One of the most powerful experiences I wrote about in my thesis was about how I once encountered the sense of being a part of something bigger through music:

> For me, certain truths have been found amongst the Neolithic people of Great Britain. Studying these people has helped me to see the truths of the human story. It has also helped me to better understand what Rob Bell calls sacred ground, which is any place where you can sense that something bigger is taking place than what is actually occurring right now in this space. I can remember feeling this at U of A Band Day my freshman year. I was in the Pride of Arizona marching band all four years of college, but during my freshman year I was not sure if I was going to march the next year or not. I was leaning towards doing it again, and then Band Day made me sure that I was going to. I remember the night show, and just sensing that I was a part of something so much

2. LeCluyse, "To Think of Time," 18–19.

bigger, bigger even than the 250-member marching band. I was a part of the music of humanity. I think that I find a similar sense when I visit these sites. They are, to me, something more than just an ancient site. They are places where people lived and worshiped, laughed, loved, and cried. They are places where people asked questions, maybe some of the same questions that I ask today.[3]

Fire, music—they are things that remind us of being on sacred ground. Several years after college, I was once again reminded of this in a fairly unexpected location, the most magical place on Earth! It wasn't through the diverse sea of people I waited in line with to ride Space Mountain or watch the fireworks, although there is a shared experience in that. It was actually the nighttime show at Disney's Epcot—*IllumiNations: Reflections of Earth*. As the show began, I was struck by the words about gathering around the fire:

> We've gathered here tonight around the fire, as people of all lands have gathered for thousands and thousands of years before us, to share the light and to share a story, an amazing story, as old as time itself, but still being written. And though each of us has our own individual stories to tell, a true adventure emerges when we bring them all together as one.[4]

What does all of this mean for us, and for our faith journeys? What does it mean to be reminded by Disney, a corporate giant, though one that does a fabulous job at storytelling, that we are all part of an amazing story that covers thousands of years, a story we remember as we gather around the fire? Why does it matter that we think about any of this?

It matters because it reminds us that we are on sacred ground, and the God of our ancestors, both biblical and otherwise, meets us on sacred ground. What does God use to get Moses' attention as he is out tending the sheep in the hills? Fire. Moses probably saw fire throughout the day everyday; it was a much more essential part of life then, but how often did he stop and notice it? That's one of the questions asked of this Scripture; was this a divine fire, completely unexpected and out of place, or was this a fire that Moses stopped and noticed, not really so extraordinary except that he actually paid attention to it? When Moses first encounters God, and

---

3. LeCluyse, "To Think of Time," 23.

4. *IllumiNations: Reflections of Earth* was the nighttime show at Disney's Epcot from 1999 until 2019. These words are from the opening narration. For a sample, see DLP Welcome, "Illuminations," 1:14.

later when Moses wonders how to tell others who this God is, God tells him that he is encountering the God of his ancestors, the God of Abraham and Sarah, Isaac and Rebecca, Jacob and Rachel; the God of his ancestors is sending him to free the Israelites. God reminds Moses that he is a part of something much larger, a story that spans generations and centuries.

Sacred ground, holy ground, isn't just the floor in churches or synagogues. It's not some place where you are required to take off your shoes. But I get why God tells Moses to take his shoes off and to really feel with his bare skin where he is, to connect with it. Sacred ground is found in places that invite us to connect to God, to the mysteries of the universe, to the story of humanity, and so much more; and the truth is, that holy ground can show up anywhere at any time that we allow ourselves to be open to it. Sometimes these are called thin spaces, spaces in which the divide between earth and the divine are especially thin. For me, the Neolithic sites of Great Britain are sacred ground, and while I once worried that some may consider that heretical, I don't anymore. Watching the waves on the beach, hiking through nature, laughing at a dinner with family or friends, are all sacred ground, opportunities to see beyond ourselves, to connect with the universal.

One final thought. After graduating from seminary, I moved to Philadelphia to begin working at the CA at the University of Pennsylvania. On one level, this was for a pretty straightforward reason—this is where I was offered a job, and it was a job that I wanted. The job description was exciting. I would get to experience living in a city (something I was looking for), and I'd be about an hour from my family for at least the next couple years. It was a great opportunity! What I didn't think about until I was here is that Philadelphia is also the city where my maternal grandmother grew up and where her family lived and worked. When I walk over to Old City, I walk by the Curtis Building, where my great-grandfather worked. When I go eat a cheesesteak at Jim's, which opened in 1939, or visit some of the city's historical sites, or go to church, I wonder if my grandmother, who passed away when I was in high school, was at these same places. So while, on one level, moving to Philly was just part of a series of events in my life, on another I was moving to a city in which I already had ancestral ties. I was moving to a place where my ancestors had lived, and somehow, I think this has made Philly have more of a sense of home for me. Maybe this was a place where knowing there were connections would remind me that I was on sacred ground, connected across time and space to those who came before me, both in this city and hundreds or thousands of years ago across the sea, and God has been present throughout it all.

Prayer

God of our ancestors,
Of our parents and grandparents,
Of those who lived on this planet before we even knew you
As we do today,
Thank you for being with us through all of human history.
In the stories of those who came before,
We find ourselves,
Friends sharing secrets, joy, and grief,
Lovers experiencing complete acceptance,
Siblings growing together,
Parents and children bonded together.
Invite us to realize how often we are on holy ground,
A space where we can experience you,
But also our connections to the human story,
A reminder that we are part of something bigger.
Help us to pause and see the fire,
And to see the role you have for us to play in this story.
Amen.

Reflection Questions

1. Where have you experienced being on sacred ground? What was that experience like?

2. Have you thought about your ancestors, either more recent or long passed? In what ways do you feel connected to them?

3. How do you feel connected to the larger story of humanity? Are there experiences or places where you have found this connection especially poignant?

Conclusion

True belonging is the spiritual practice of believing in and belonging to yourself so deeply that you can share your most authentic self with the world and find sacredness in both being a part of something and standing alone in the wilderness. True belonging doesn't require you to change who you are; it requires you to be who you are.

—Brené Brown

Our deepest fear is not that we are inadequate. Our deepest fear is that we are powerful beyond measure. It is our light, not our darkness that most frightens us. We ask ourselves, Who am I to be brilliant, gorgeous, talented, and fabulous? Actually, who are you not to be? You are a child of God. Your playing small does not serve the world. There is nothing enlightened about shrinking so that other people will not feel insecure around you. We are all meant to shine, as children do. We were born to make manifest the glory of God that is within us. It is not just in some of us; it is in everyone and as we let our own light shine, we unconsciously give others permission to do the same. As we are liberated from our own fear, our presence automatically liberates others.

—Marianne Williamson

Scripture

Therefore I tell you, do not worry about your life, what you will eat or what you will drink, or about your body, what you will wear. Is not life more than food, and the body more than clothing? Look at the birds of the air; they neither sow nor reap nor gather into barns, and yet your heavenly Father feeds them. Are you not of

Conclusion

more value than they? And can any of you by worrying add a single hour to your span of life? And why do you worry about clothing? Consider the lilies of the field, how they grow; they neither toil nor spin, yet I tell you, even Solomon in all his glory was not clothed like one of these. But if God so clothes the grass of the field, which is alive today and tomorrow is thrown into the oven, will he not much more clothe you—you of little faith? Therefore do not worry, saying, "What will we eat?" or "What will we drink?" or "What will we wear?" For it is the Gentiles who strive for all these things; and indeed your heavenly Father knows that you need all these things. But strive first for the kingdom of God and [God's] righteousness, and all these things will be given to you as well.

So do not worry about tomorrow, for tomorrow will bring worries of its own. Today's trouble is enough for today. (Matt 6:25–34)

ONE OF THE SCARIEST things for me about writing this book is that if I was going to do it well, do it in a way that hopefully helped others to feel like they truly aren't the only one, I had to be vulnerable. I needed to open myself up and share some of the parts of my story that I hold dear and treasure, but also some of the parts of myself and my life that I am less proud of and some things that still can feel kind of raw. My hope is that in doing so, you were able to explore your life and experiences and feel seen.

I'm realizing that I have now spent over half of my life based in a higher education setting. I clearly find deep joy and satisfaction in working with those in undergraduate and graduate programs, who are in this period of development that shapes us in so many ways. I also believe that our faith is meant to play a substantial role in it all, but that we don't always have the resources to make this happen in ways that feel authentic to our faith. I hope this book can be one of these resources for you.

I know I haven't covered everything in these pages. We each will have a unique college experience. There are of course a few stories I chose to keep, memories that I want to be mine to hold.

Wherever you are at in your college journey as you read this conclusion, I hope that you can make the most of whatever time you have left in this experience. I may not ever refer to it as the best four years of your life, but it is certainly a unique time. In many settings, it provides you with so many opportunities to learn and grow and explore right at your fingertips. It may take you time to find your people, but they are probably there, somewhere, and they will hopefully be some of your people for life. Mine are. I've been texting with a couple of them recently about a new movie that brought back memories from our college days.

I hope that you know you are a beloved child of God. *God loves you no matter what.* No matter what grades you get or what you decide to do with your life or who you discover you are, God loves you. *Rest in that knowledge, now and always.*

I leave you with the words that began the conclusion of my college thesis: "So I go forth, living one day at I time. Whatever I go through, I know that I am not the first, nor will I be the last. I know that I am a part of a sacred story, where there is something so much bigger going on."[1] Go forth to love and serve God in all that you do. Live your part of the story, becoming the person God has created you to be.

---

1. LeCluyse, "To Think of Time," 25.

Bibliography

Aneja, Geeta. "By Our Love." Around the Table. https://aroundthetableca.blogspot.com/2013/11/by-our-love.html.

Bell, Rob. *Velvet Elvis*. Grand Rapids: Zondervan, 2005.

Buber, Martin. *I and Thou*. Translated by Walter Kaufmann. New York. Touchstone, 1970.

Buechner, Frederick. *Whistling in the Dark: A Doubter's Dictionary*. New York: HarperCollins, 1993.

Childers, Jana. *Birthing the Sermon: Women Preachers on the Creative Process*. Atlanta: Chalice, 2001.

DLP Welcome. "Illuminations: Reflections of Earth—EPCOT." https://www.youtube.com/watch?v=hJzn_M92Uus.

Friends of Peace Pilgrim, ed. *Peace Pilgrim: Her Life and Work in Her Own Words*. Shelton, CT: Friends of Peace Pilgrim, 2004.

Iyer, Pico. "Where Is Home?" TED. June 2013. https://www.ted.com/talks/pico_iyer_where_is_home.

Kaplan, Alyssa. "Proclaiming God's Love." Around the Table. https://aroundthetableca.blogspot.com/2014/04/proclaiming-gods-love-by-alyssa-kaplan.html.

Kershner, Irvin, dir. *Star Wars: Episode V—The Empire Strikes Back*. San Francisco, CA: Lucasfilm, 1980.

Lamott, Anne. *Plan B: Further Thoughts on Faith*. New York: Penguin, 2006.

LeCluyse, Megan. "To Think of Time: The Role of Neolithic Sites in My Spiritual Journey." BA thesis, University of Arizona, 2008.

Lewis, C. S. *The Lion, the Witch, and the Wardrobe*. New York: HarperTrophy, 1950.

Miller, Donald. *Blue Like Jazz*. Nashville: Thomas Nelson, 2003.

Musker, John, and Ron Clements, dirs. *Moana*. Burbank, CA: Walt Disney Animation Studios, 2016.

Parker, Palmer. J. *Let Your Life Speak: Listening for the Voice of Vocation*. San Francisco: Jossey-Bass, 2024.

Rohr, Richard. *Soul Brothers: Men in the Bible Speak to Men Today*. Maryknoll, NY: Orbis, 2004.

Rowling, J. K. *Harry Potter and the Sorcerer's Stone*. New York: Scholastic, 1998.

Rumi. *Open Secret: Versions of Rumi*. Translated by Coleman Barks and John Moyne. Boulder, CO: Shambala, 1999.

Sesame Street. "Ernie Learns to Put Down the Duckie." https://www.youtube.com/watch?v=acBixR_JRuM.

Bibliography

Sharpsteen, Ben, et al., dirs. *Pinocchio*. Burbank, CA: Walt Disney Productions, 1940.
Silverstein, Shel. *Falling Up*. New York: Harper, 1996.
Williamson, Marianne. *A Return to Love*. New York: HarperCollins, 1996.

www.ingramcontent.com/pod-product-compliance
Lightning Source LLC
Chambersburg PA
CBHW072132160426
43197CB00012B/2080